God Is for You

GOD IS FOR YOU

· D E L O S · M I L E S ·

BROADMAN PRESS
Nashville, Tennessee

4250-58

ISBN: 0-8654-5058-0

Dewey Decimal Classification: 158

Subject Heading: PSYCHOLOGY, APPLIED CHRISTIAN LIFE

Library of Congress Catalog Number: 88-35287

Printed in the United States of America

Library of Congress Cataloging-in-Publication Data

Miles, Delos.
  God is for you.

  Bibliography: p.
  1. Bible—Study. 2. Need (Psychology) I. Title.
BS600.2.M53 1989   220'.076   88-35287
ISBN 0-8054-5058-0

To the memory of Dallas Miles,
Who was twice my brother
And a deacon who fervently loved
And faithfully served the
God of the Bible.

Contents

Preface

A friend of W. C. Fields once walked into his dressing room unannounced and caught him reading the Bible. Knowing Fields's cynical attitude toward religion, the friend was surprised. Fields himself seemed embarrassed and quickly shut the Book: "Just looking for loopholes," he explained.

Whether you are just looking for loopholes like W. C. Fields or looking for something else, the Bible is for all persons who can read. It is a today Book.

My purpose is to show how we can meet many of our own life needs, and those of others, through personal Bible study. Twenty-six common human needs are dealt with, from the most basic needs for food and water to the higher needs for recognition and meaning.

Readers familiar with the writings of psychologist Abraham H. Maslow will recognize my indebtedness to Maslow's hierarchy of needs. Insofar as possible, I have sought to organize the book's structure and outline around Maslow's seminal work on motivation.

Maslow was, of course, not a Christian. Yet he openly recognized the need for the transcendent and the transpersonal in his writings. In fact, he went so far as to say that without this dimension in our lives, "We get sick, violent, and nihilistic, or else hopeless and apathetic."

You are entitled to know that I identify Maslow's transcendent and transpersonal dimension of reality with the God of the Bible. As Blaise Pascal, a famous French philosopher of the seventeenth century, observed: the God of the Bible is "the God of Abraham, Isaac, and Jacob," and not the god of the philosophers and sages.

Insomuch as the ability lies within me, I have self-consciously tried to design these Bible studies for laypersons who like the Bible but who may not yet care for the church. Nonetheless, since all human beings have essentially the same basic needs, whatever their faith orientation may or may not be, I should be quite surprised if these studies did not help both Christians and not-yet Christians.

Each of the twenty-six studies is written so as to stand on its own. You may, therefore, start with any chapter or read only those chapters which appear to deal with your needs at that time. Each study is similarly arranged around two Scripture selections from both the Old and New Testaments. The printed Scripture text is included for your convenience and for immediate reference. It is from *The Good News Bible,* The Bible in Today's English Version. Incidentally, Scriptures that appear as poetry will have slash marks at the end of a line where the line ends in the source.

Along with this book, you need only a copy of the Bible in order to do this kind of personal Bible study. While your Bible may be in any version, *The Good News Bible* might be more useful to you since these studies are geared to that text. If you have access to a Bible concordance and/or a Bible dictionary, you can find opportunities to use them, but those tools are not essential to these studies.

One of my goals has been to write the studies without using many theological code words, without imposing heavy religious language on readers. Another goal has been to write without using encumbering footnotes and endnotes.

For those of you who would like to do further Bible study on your own, and need more tools to employ in your search, I recommend the *Disciple's Study Bible* produced by Holman Bible Publishers in 1988 and available through most book stores.

I am particularly indebted to several persons for their assistance with this volume. My wife, Nada, typed the first draft of several of the earlier chapters, proofed the entire manuscript, and assisted me with gathering some of the illustrations used. She has been my partner in this labor as in all of my work. Judy Durham, my faculty secretary, has graciously and quickly processed all of these words. My editor at Broadman Press has made many helpful suggestions and been so kind as to read and critique some of the first drafts of several chapters.

While I have had the advantage of learning from many of my students, three of them who have taught me the most about meeting persons at their points of need are Donald J. Christian, William H. Denning, and Dane M. Blankenship. Each of these men is skilled in meeting human needs after the servant model of Jesus Christ.

PART I
PHYSIOLOGICAL NEEDS

1

The Need for Food

Reliable estimates are that twenty-eight persons die as a consequence of hunger every minute of every hour of every day, and twenty-one of those are children. That adds up to fourteen million tragic deaths a year.

Probably the darkest cloud on the world horizon is hunger. Exact figures are hard to secure, but Jean Mayer, nutritionist at Harvard University, and the United Nations Food and Agriculture Organization (FAO) agree that around a billion people suffer from lack of food; four-hundred million are at the edge of starvation. It is estimated that some fifteen million of these are in the United States. We are informed that every day more than twelve thousand people die of starvation, and the numbers increase as population grows.

More than six-hundred thousand of the world's citizens exist on incomes of less than fifty dollars per year. What is life like for the extremely poor of the world? Take the example of the Abdul Halim family in Bangladesh. The Halims have four children. Abdul neither reads nor writes. He has no problem with hard work, when he can find it, and provided he has sufficient strength to work. Abdul would never dream of three good meals a day.

He owns a small plot of land, less than one fourth of an acre. That makes him more prosperous than thirty-five thousand other Bangladeshis who own no land.

This family of six must be content with a meal of rice, occasionally served with a small portion of lentil soup but usually with only a few hot peppers and some fried greens. A glass of milk is beyond their expectation. If the Halim family can manage this meal twice a day, and if there is work, they can survive.

The story of the Halim family of Bangladesh might be told of many other countries. Only the names and numbers would change. Glance at Brazil for a moment. Not long ago it was reported that 80 percent of the children in Brazil suffer from malnutrition, that twenty-five million children were living in the streets, and one thousand children die daily from starvation.

A 1988 article in *Newsweek* reported 9.7 million impoverished rural Americans and called this widely dispersed underclass "America's Third World." That article went on to say that many of the rural poor drift like dry leaves across the landscape, their only legacy being the poverty which they pass from one generation to another.

Yet, in spite of the poverty in America—both rural and urban—in comparison with the rest of the world, we are a rich nation. We Americans have less than 6 percent of the world's population, but consume 35 percent of the world's resources. Someone has calculated that if the world were a global village of 100 people:

- Seventy would be unable to read;
- One would have a college education
- Fifty would suffer from malnutrition
- Eighty would live in substandard housing by American standards
- Six would be Americans, and they would have over half of the town's entire income.

Scripture Selections

Psalm 78:18-20

[18]They deliberately put God to the test/by demanding the food they wanted./[19]They spoke against God and said,/"Can God supply food in the desert?/[20]It is true that he struck the rock,/and water flowed out in a torrent;/but can he also provide us with bread/and give his people meat?"

John 6:5-15

⁵Jesus looked around and saw that a large crowd was coming to him, so he asked Philip, "Where can we buy enough food to feed all these people?" (⁶He said this to test Philip; actually he already knew what he would do.)

⁷Philip answered, "For everyone to have even a little, it would take more than two hundred silver coins to buy enough bread."

⁸Another one of his disciples, Andrew, who was Simon Peter's brother, said, ⁹"There is a boy here who has five loaves of barley bread and two fish. But they will certainly not be enough for all these people."

¹⁰"Make the people sit down." Jesus told them. (There was a lot of grass there.) So all the people sat down; there were about five thousand men. ¹¹Jesus took the bread, gave thanks to God, and distributed it to the people who were sitting there. He did the same with the fish, and they all had as much as they wanted. ¹²When they were all full, he said to his disciples, "Gather the pieces left over; let us not waste a bit." ¹³So they gathered them all and filled twelve baskets with the pieces left over from the five barley loaves which the people had eaten.

¹⁴Seeing this miracle that Jesus had performed, the people there said, "Surely this is the Prophet who was to come into the world!" ¹⁵Jesus knew that they were about to come and seize him in order to make him king by force; so he went off again to the hills by himself.

Comments on Scripture Selection

Psalms 136:25 says of God, "He gives food to every living creature;/his love is eternal." Twenty-six times in that psalm the phrase "his love is eternal" is repeated. Part of the proof that God loved Israel with an everlasting love was that He gave her the food she needed even during her desert wanderings of forty years. That is the specific point to which Psalm 78:18-20 refers. Read Exodus 16:1-36 and Numbers 11:4-35 in order to see how God supplied Israel with "food in the desert" (Ps. 78:19).

The food which God regularly provided was called "manna." "It was like a small white seed, and tasted like thin cakes made with honey" (Ex. 16:31). A fuller description of manna may be found in Numbers 11:7-9.

Manna was the "bread" mentioned in Psalm 78:20. But what was the "meat" referred to in that verse? It was the quail described in Numbers 11:31-32.

Israel's two questions to God in Psalm 78:19 and 20 may, therefore, be answered: "Yes, He can." God actually "spread a table in the wilderness" (Ps. 78:19, RSV) for His people Israel.

John 6:5-15 is no less remarkable. The food (see v. 5) turned out to be a boy's lunch of five small barley loaves and two fish (v. 9). The miracle was that Jesus fed about five thousand men (v. 10) with that lad's lunch. When they were all full, His disciples filled twelve baskets with the left over pieces (v. 13). Not a bit was wasted.

However, one problem did develop from the feeding of the five thousand. The people were about to seize Jesus and make Him their king by force. Did they make the mistake of thinking that there must be a free lunch after all?

Questions to Think About

• How did God show His love for the nation Israel in Psalm 78:18-20, and how did Jesus show His compassion for the five thousand in John 6?

• Do I think God is just as concerned for the Abdul Halim families of this world as He was for the nation Israel and as Jesus was for the five thousand?

• If I am one of those six Americans living in this global village, what is my particular responsibility to the fifty global citizens of my village who suffer from malnutrition?

• Am I motivated to feed the hungry because of what I am going to get, or because of what I have already gotten?

• The multitudes of John 6 wanted a free lunch from Jesus (see John 6:14-15). Is there really such a thing as a free lunch in the world?

Conclusion

A teenage girl in Greenville, North Carolina, fasts one day each month in order to do something about world hunger. She also coordinates the world hunger project in her community.

If we say, "I'm not responsible for the Abdul Halims," James 2:14-17 says we are responsible. Also, 1 John 3:17 says that's no way to treat a needy person.

John's Gospel never has a deed like the feeding of the five thousand without a corresponding word to go with that deed. The word which explains that deed is found in John 6:35.

2

The Need for Water

"Land is the mother, and water is her blood." The first time I ever read that quotation, I had to do a double take on it. I think it was no accident that this quote first impressed me in Santa Fe, New Mexico, where the annual waterfall is not nearly so plentiful as it is back East where I was born and reared.

The great droughts of 1986 and 1988 in the American Southeast and Midwest made many of us more aware of the value of water. The 1988 drought savagely underscored the absolute necessity of H^2O (the chemical formula for water) for human survival. That year may be remembered as the year of droughts, global warming trends, and ozone holes in the earth's atmosphere.

Life as we know it, in all of its life forms, simply cannot exist apart from water. The United States Agriculture Department predicted that because of drought the US grain harvest in 1988 would be 31 percent less than in 1987. That meant that our 1988 harvest would be the smallest since 1970. Approximately twenty-two hundred US counties lost crops and income because of the 1988 drought.

International grain stockpiles in 1988 showed their sharpest one-year drop since such records have been kept. The grain reserve needed to feed the world was reliably predicted to fall from 101 days to 54 days by the beginning of 1990. Food scarcity and higher food prices may well dominate the 1990s. The biggest culprit is worldwide drought.

Coupled with the pressing need for water itself is the special need for *clean* water. Even as I write this, a smattering of medical waste has washed ashore on the beaches of Bogue Banks in North Carolina. While the navy has taken responsibility for the syringes, vials, and other debris washed ashore at Indian Beach and Atlantic Beach, that does not calm North Carolinians who cannot help fearing for their own precious coast.

Some beaches in the northeast were closed all summer (1988) because of a vile assault of medical garbage and sewage. Apparently the ocean is being treated as a liquid landfill. Hypodermic needles on the sand, globs of sewage in the surf, dead dolphins along the US coast, and over seven thousand dead harbor seals in the North and Baltic Seas testify to the alarming need for unpolluted water.

Scripture Selection

Numbers 20:2-11

[2]There was no water where they camped, so the people gathered around Moses and Aaron [3]and complained: "It would have been better if we had died in front of the Lord's Tent along with our fellow Israelites. [4]Why have you brought us out into this wilderness? Just so that we can die here with our animals? [5]Why did you bring us out of Egypt into this miserable place where nothing will grow? There's no grain, no figs, no grapes, no pomegranates. There is not even any water to drink!" [6] Moses and Aaron moved away from the people and stood at the entrance of the Tent. They bowed down with their faces

to the ground, and the dazzling light of the Lord's presence appeared to them.

[7]The Lord said to Moses, [8]"Take the stick that is in front of the Covenant Box, and then you and Aaron assemble the whole community. There in front of them all speak to that rock over there, and water will gush out of it. In this way you will bring water out of the rock for the people, for them and their animals to drink." [9]Moses went and got the stick, as the Lord had commanded.

[10]He and Aaron assembled the whole community in front of the rock, and Moses said, "Listen, you rebels! Do we have to get water out of this rock for you?" Then Moses raised the stick and struck the rock twice with it, and a great stream of water gushed out, and all the people and animals drank.

John 4:5-15

[5]In Samaria he came to a town named Sychar, which was not far from the field that Jacob had given to his son Joseph. [6]Jacob's well was there, and Jesus, tired out by the trip, sat down by the well. It was about noon.

[7]A Samaritan woman came to draw some water, and Jesus said to her, "Give me a drink of water." ([8]His disciples had gone into town to buy food.)

[9]The woman answered, "You are a Jew, and I am a Samaritan—so how can you ask me for a drink?" (Jews will not use the same cups and bowls that Samaritans use.)

[10]Jesus answered, "If you only knew what God gives and who it is that is asking you for a drink, you would ask him, and he would give you life-giving water.

[11]"Sir," the woman said, "you don't have a bucket, and the well is deep. Where would you get that life-giving water? [12]It was our ancestor Jacob who gave us this well; he and his sons and his flocks all drank from it. You don't claim to be greater than Jacob, do you?"

[13]Jesus answered, "Whoever drinks this water will get thirsty again. [14]but whoever drinks the water that I will give him will never

be thirsty again. The water that I will give him will become in him a spring which will provide him with life-giving water and give him eternal life."

¹⁵"Sir," the woman said, "give me that water! Then I will never be thirsty again, nor will I have to come here to draw water."

Comments on Scripture Selection

The miracle of water from the rock parallels what appears to be the same story in Exodus 17:1-7. Although the setting of the stories is different, the name Meribah, meaning "complaining," appears in both versions (Ex. 17:7; Num. 20:13).

God not only fed His people with manna and quail (Ex. 16:1-36), He also gave them and their animals clean water to drink during their wilderness wanderings. Verses 2-5 of Numbers 20 describe the complaint of the people of Israel against Moses and Aaron, their leaders. Verses 6-8 reveal God's answer to their complaint, an answer which came through Moses. Verses 9-11 are an account of how God gave water to His people and their animals.

The "Tent" of verse 6 was the temporary worship center which God commanded Moses to build for the nation Israel during her wilderness wanderings. The "stick" of verses 7 and 11 was Aaron's famous walking stick (Num. 17:1-13). The "Covenant Box" of verse 7 was the ark of the covenant (Ex. 25:10-22) which contained "the gold jar with the manna in it, Aaron's stick that had sprouted leaves, and the two stone tablets with the commandments written on them" (Heb. 9:4). In short, this special "Box" held a sample of the food which God fed Israel in her desert wanderings, Aaron's miraculous rod, and the Ten Commandments.

Compare the Old and New Testament selections. Note that in Numbers 20 the people of Israel complainingly requested water of their leaders, whereas in John 4 Jesus courteously requested water from a Samaritan woman (see vv. 7-9). Samaritans and Jews had no social dealings with each other, yet Jesus was not prejudiced against this woman because of her race, sex, religion, or morals.

The conversation between Jesus and the Samaritan woman shifts in verses 10-15 to an offer of "life-giving water." This "life-giving water" which Jesus offered was even more miraculous than that which God gave to Israel at Kadesh. Perhaps we should not be at all surprised that the one being offered such thirst-quenching water had difficulty understanding exactly what kind of water this kind Jewish man was talking about.

Questions to Think About

• In what sense may water be said to be the blood of "mother Earth?"

• Genesis 2:10 says "A stream flowed in Eden and watered the garden"; whereas, Revelation 22:1 and 2 refer to "the river of the water of life, sparkling like crystal, and coming from the throne of God and of the Lamb and flowing down the middle of the city's street." Do I see any significance to the Bible's opening with a stream in the garden of Eden and closing with a river in the new Jerusalem (see also Rev. 21:2)?

• Do I believe God is as concerned for my thirst and for the thirst of others as He was for the thirst of His people Israel at Kadesh in Numbers 20?

• What does the thirst of Jesus in John 4 tell me about the humanity of Jesus?

• Along with my continuing need for water, like the woman at the well, are there some other needs and wants that I have which I can name?

Conclusion

Tim Diamond of Juneau, Alaska, is exporting ice to Japan. The ice comes from glacial icebergs. Japanese gourmet shops sell these bluish ice chips for $1.50 a pound. Formed under a glacier's tremendous weight, this ice is dense—only 20 percent air as compared to the usual 75 percent. Therefore, it lasts much longer than tap-water cubes. Diamond's ice-exporting company likes to boast that the ice is probably as pure as anything on earth, although it may not be as ancient as ads claim, since glaciers are continuously being renewed by rain and snow.

Isaiah 55:1 and Revelation 22:17 advertise a different kind of water which customers who have tried it claim to be older, purer, more refreshing, and more lasting than glacier water. God knows that we can't live life at its fullest without both the water for which Jesus thirsted and the water which Jesus offered to quench our thirst.

3

The Need for Rest

"George Washington Slept Here." How many times have you seen that sign posted on antique inns and famous, old houses? I've seen it so often that I find myself wondering if George Washington really did sleep in all those places. But one thing is for sure: even presidents need to rest just like everybody else.

One night when William Howard Taft was president of the United States, he got very tired. He went outside and looked at the stars for a long time. Then he said to himself, *OK, now that you know how insignificant you are, you can go on back inside and go back to work.*

Sleep and respite from labor aren't by any means the only kind of rest we need. We need rest from much of the noise around us. Sometimes we may surely feel that the world is a big mouth where everybody talks, but few listen. While we may agree with Winston Churchill's quaint phrase that "to jaw-jaw is better than to war-war," that doesn't prevent us from lamenting what someone else called "the long littleness of these passing days."

You and I live in a world which makes it hard to plan for the final rest that should come in one's own cemetery plot. Did you hear what happened to Mattie Dudley of Charlottesville, Virginia? Dudley earns about five dollars per week selling newspapers on the street. Her atrophied legs put her in a wheelchair early in life. Until recently, she had been scraping by on $284.30 a month in Supplemental Security income.

Then, Dudley was accused of violating regulations that confine SSI payments to persons with assets of fifteen-hundred dollars or less. It turned out that she had a one-thousand-dollar burial certificate which she purchased in 1979. Interest on that certificate put her over the limitations on total assets. Only time will tell whether this tangle of regulations will be changed to accommodate Dudley and others similarly situated.

What some of us need is refuge from the dizzying pace of change in the world. Professor A. C. Reid, when in his nineties, told how as a young man it took him twenty-two hours to come from his father's farm near Lexington, North Carolina, to Wake Forest College in Wake Forest, NC. He traveled by train and had to flag down the train as it passed by his dad's farm, go to Lexington and change trains there, go to Greensboro and change trains there, go to Raleigh and change trains there for the final leg of his journey to Wake Forest. Dr. Reid smiled and said: "My son a few weeks ago ate breakfast in Paris, France, and ate lunch in New York City." In about seventy years or so, that's how much travel has changed.

Scripture Selection

Psalms 127:1-2

[1]If the LORD does not build the house,/the work of the builders is useless;/if the Lord does not protect the city,/it does no good for the sentries to stand guard./[2]It is useless to work so hard for a living,/getting up early and going to bed late./For the Lord provides for those he loves,/while they are asleep.

Matthew 11:28-30

[28]"Come to me, all of you who are tired from carrying heavy loads, and I will give you rest. [29]Take my yoke and put it on you, and learn from me, because I am gentle and humble in spirit; and you will find rest. [30]For the yoke I will give you is easy, and the load I will put on you is light."

Comments on Scripture Selection

Psalm 127 is a good example of what is called wisdom writing in the Hebrew songbook. Read Psalms 1, 49, 73, and 128 to get a better feel for such writing. These wisdom writings seek to teach principles and practices which, when faithfully followed, brings the greatest happiness in this life. Their point of view is more this-worldly than otherworldly, and more in tune with laypersons than with the professionally religious.

This psalm falls into two parts, verses 1-2 and verses 3-5. The two parts of Psalm 127 are tied together around the overall theme of the vanity of human efforts without God. Four common human interests which we dare not pursue apart from God are mentioned by the psalmist: building a house (v. 1), watching over a city (v. 1), working hard for a living (v. 2), and building a family (vv. 3-5).

Focus especially upon verse 2. The Hebrew text for this verse is uncertain, a fact which accounts for some differences in its translation, particularly with regards to the word *asleep* in *The Good News Bible*. The *New International Version* translates verse 2, "In vain you rise early/ and stay up late,/toiling for food to eat—/for he grants sleep to those he loves."

A farmer who works long hours of toil in the fields, from early in the morning until late in the evening, is the kind of person the psalmist wrote about. Farmers, back then, ate their chief meal at the end of the day. These words do not belittle hard work. Rather, they say that no matter how industrious is the worker, it is God who makes such labor fruitful and who gives sleep and rest to the laborer.

The yoke of Matthew 11:28-30 was the specially fitted piece of wood which enabled oxen to pull such heavy loads. The "heavy loads" of verse 28 may refer to the burdens put upon the people by some of the religious leaders of Jesus' nation. All those who are "tired from carrying heavy loads," whatever their burdens may be, are invited to yoke themselves up with Jesus. The yoke Jesus puts on persons is easier than that of the legalistic religion taught by the scribes and Pharisees (see Mark 7:2-5,8; Acts 15:10). His burdens are also lighter than the burdens others put on us.

Questions to Think About

• In the light of Psalms 127:2, can I afford to leave God out of my plans for sleep and rest?

• Do I believe that God not only provides sleep for me, but that He also provides for me while I sleep?

• Can "rest" be understood in Matthew 11:28-30 to mean not merely the absence of labor, hardship, and suffering, but also the absence of guilt, worry, anxiety, and lack of meaning?

• Am I yoked up with somebody whose yoke is "easy" and whose load is "light" (see Matt. 11:30)?

• What can I do to help the Mattie Dudleys of this world?

• What can I do to ease the load of those persons who are worn out and put out with so much change in their daily life?

Conclusion

Standing within the main entrance of Johns Hopkins Hospital in Baltimore is a famous statue of Jesus Christ. It stands across the main corridor to the hospital, as if placed there to compel everyone to stop and take notice. Those who gain entrance must walk to the left or right around that large figure which fills the space even to the high ceiling. The hands of Jesus are outstretched, and as your face looks into the face of the statue, He seems to be repeating His words chiseled into the marble below: "Come unto Me, all ye that labor and are heavily laden, and I will give you rest."

4

The Need for Healing

How would you like to live your whole life in such pain and discomfort that you think if you can just make it through *this* night you might live through another day? What purpose might there be in that kind of suffering?

"My whole life I've heard doctors say, 'If she makes it through the night she'll be OK.' " So spoke Meg Coker of Pineville, Arkansas.*

Born in 1913, Coker was reared on a farm. At the age of four Meg fell off the hay wagon. The heavy iron wheels ran over one leg and broke it. When she was twelve, a tendon in her other leg was severed by an old-fashioned corn cutter. Back then, doctors traveled by horse and buggy. When the doctor finally arrived at Meg's home to treat her, he operated on her on the kitchen table by the light of coal oil lamps.

Meg's most serious childhood illness came at the age of fourteen when she contracted scarlet fever. The fever damaged her ears, requiring her to see a specialist for eight years. Also the fever damaged Meg's heart.

Coker recovered enough to continue her schooling and to get married. She became the proud mother of two daughters, who gave her five grandchildren and two great grandchildren. One of her great joys has been the love of her family.

But Coker's damaged heart has continued to plague her. Today she

(*Because this is a true story, name and place have been changed to protect individuals involved.)

suffers from angina pectoris, a disease characterized by insufficient supply of oxygen to the heart, resulting in heart pains. She has had four heart attacks, and been confined to her bed since the age of forty-eight. In 1985 she suffered a stroke and temporarily lost her speech and use of one side of her body.

Another heavy blow hit Coker in 1984 when her husband of fifty-four years died of cancer.

Coker does not talk about her lifelong afflictions in order to evoke sympathy. Nor does she cite her troubles as a bitter reminder of what might have been. During one illness, she confessed that she felt tempted to give up, and suicide seemed a simple way out. "The devil was after me, and I wanted to kill myself," said Coker. It was at that time, as a fully grown adult, that she turned her pain over to God. "I turned my life over to the Lord," continued Coker, "and told Him I would take whatever was put on me. . . . I had such peace."

Today Coker takes life one day at a time. Every day she thanks the Lord for new strength. One of her daughters, reflecting on her mother's sufferings, noted that God's purpose for her mother's life was to be a "witness to anyone who is ill."

Scripture Selection

Isaiah 53:4-5

[4]"But he endured the suffering/that should have been ours,/the pain that we should have borne./All the while we thought that his suffering/was punishment sent by God./[5]But because of our sins he was wounded,/beaten because of the evil we did./We are healed by the punishment he suffered,/made whole by the blows he received."

Mark 5:25-34

[25]There was a woman who had suffered terribly from severe bleeding for twelve years, [26]even though she had been treated by many doctors. She had spent all her money, but instead of getting better she got worse all the time. [27]She had heard about Jesus, so she came

in the crowd behind him, ²⁸saying to herself, "If I just touch his clothes, I will get well."

²⁹She touched his cloak, and her bleeding stopped at once; and she had the feeling inside herself that she was healed of her trouble. ³⁰At once Jesus knew that power had gone out of him, so he turned around in the crowd and asked, "Who touched my clothes?"

³¹His disciples answered, "You see how the people are crowding you; why do you ask who touched you?"

³²But Jesus kept looking around to see who had done it. ³³The woman realized what had happened to her, so she came, trembling with fear, knelt at his feet, and told him the whole truth. ³⁴Jesus said to her, "My daughter, your faith has made you well. Go in peace, and be healed of your trouble."

Comments on Scripture Selection

The verses from Isaiah 53 are from one of four or five such poems or songs found in the second half of the Book of Isaiah (see Isa. 42:1-4; 49:1-6; 50:4-9; 52:13 to 53:12; and 61:1-3). They are called "servant songs" or "servant poems" because they are about God's servant. Bible scholars differ on whether the servant of the Lord is the nation Israel, a faithful remnant of the nation Israel, or a particular person in Israel.

The Revised Standard Version of the first half of Isaiah 53:4 reads, "Surely he has borne our griefs/and carried our sorrows." Therefore, "the suffering that should have been ours" is a reference to our griefs, our infirmities, and our sicknesses. Also, "the pain we should have borne" is a reference to our sorrows, our pains, and our diseases.

Isaiah pointed in these verses to a loving Suffering Servant whom God would provide as a sacrifice for sin. The personal pronouns of vv. 4-6 indicate that the Servant is neither the nation Israel, the faithful remnant of the nation Israel, nor the prophet himself. The New Testament identifies Him as Jesus Christ (see 1 Pet. 2:21-25).

When we come to the healing of a woman who had suffered terribly from severe bleeding for twelve years in Mark 5, we may see why someone has called Jesus Christ the hinge between the Old and

New Testaments. The same Servant referred to in Isaiah 53 revealed Himself as the Great Physician in the New Testament. Indeed, the Gospel of Matthew says of Him in two places, "Jesus went around visiting all the towns and villages. . . . and healed people with every kind of disease and sickness" (9:35; 4:23).

Jesus frequently healed persons of physical diseases and infirmities throughout His public ministry. He gave sight to the blind, hearing to the deaf, cleansed lepers, and made the lame walk (Matt. 11:5). These healings, along with His other miracles such as casting out demons and raising the dead, were signs pointing to the presence and power of the rule of God in His own life and ministry (see Luke 11:14-23). These deeds of Jesus were proofs that He was the long-awaited and anointed Deliverer of whom the prophets of Israel had foretold (see Mal. 4:2).

One unique feature in the example of the bleeding woman is that it is a story within a story, a case within a case, a happening within a happening, an account within an account, and a cure within a cure. Read Mark 5:21-24 and 35-43 to see how Jesus healed this woman while enroute to heal the twelve-year-old daughter of Jairus. That may well be the most unusual feature of this healing story. Surely Jesus did, as Peter said, go "everywhere, doing good and healing all" (Acts 10:38).

By letting the woman touch Him, Jesus broke a great taboo. This woman, whose menstrual bleeding had gone on for twelve years without ceasing, was ritually unclean according to her religion. Anyone who touched her or was touched by her was also automatically unclean. They would, according to the law of Moses, have to go through prescribed cleansing procedures. Yet, there is no record—not even a hint—that Jesus stopped to follow the law before healing this lady. Instead He followed the higher law of love and violated the great blood taboo.

Questions to Think About

• Is there some sense in which I may say God healed Meg Coker? If so, in what sense was she healed? If not, why the negative answer?

• Is it God's will to literally and physically heal every sick person of every illness?

• What similarities and differences do I find between the story of the bleeding woman and the story of Meg Coker?

• As I compare Mark 5:25-34 with parallel accounts of the healing of the bleeding woman in Matthew 9:20-22 and Luke 8:43-48, do I find any evidence that medical doctors are being "put down" in the story?

• What indications of the woman's faith (see v. 34) can I point to in Mark 5:25-34?

• How central is faith in healing stories, both ancient and contemporary?

• How does my story relate'to the story of Meg Coker, and to the woman with the constant issue of blood?

Conclusion

The story within a story of Mark 5 shows us that Jesus never got too busy to heal a sick person. This woman was lonely, desperate, broke, weak, and at her wits end as to what to do. When she reached out to Jesus, she was richly rewarded.

On the other hand, the story of Meg Coker shows us that God doesn't always choose to heal us of all our physical pains and troubles. We may go through each night thinking if we can get through *this* night we might live through another day. But can we live with the answer God gave to the apostle Paul about his painful physical ailment, "My grace is all you need, for my power is strongest when you are weak" (2 Cor. 12:9)?

PART II
SAFETY NEEDS

5

The Need for Shelter

Why do you think wild birds would wander confusedly in and out of a boy's hand?

When Paul Landrey was a boy, a devastating cyclone swept through the west Indian town of Dandhi-Maroli, 100 miles north of Bombay where he lived with his parents. Paul's home, made of brick and stucco, survived. All around his house, however, entire neighborhoods vanished.

The morning after the storm passed, Paul went outside. He began helping his father clear away the massive coconut and banyan trees blown down by the winds. It seemed as if every twisted branch he removed uncovered a shivering and terrified bird. For years Paul had watched those same birds make a hasty retreat to the treetops every time he approached. Yet after the storm destroyed their home, these same birds wandered confusedly in and out of Paul's hand.

Surely that was peculiar behavior for birds, don't you think? Nonetheless, reacting strangely whenever shelter is absent or inadequate is a common trait among all living creatures—persons included.

Consider the strange behavior of a boy in Pasadena, California a few years ago. The lad was in a summer tutoring program for disadvantaged children. One day while sharing in the program, he fell off a bicycle and cut his knee. The program directors insisted on going home with him to explain the accident to his mother. He stubbornly refused to allow the adult directors to take him home. Finally, they got the boy into a car for the short trip to his house.

As the tutors drove, they thought to themselves how strange it was for a child to resist their visit so strongly. One of them even remembered delightful childhood afternoons marked by a host of neighborhood playmates joining him in his room.

The injured boy asked the workers to stop the car in front of an ordinary house. Rather than leading them to the front door, the boy led them to his house in the back. It was a crumbling lean-to, rivaling anything they had seen in other huge urban slums. The walls were a combination of cardboard, tin, and splintered plywood. A broken Styrofoam ice chest served as a refrigerator. The only source of running water was a garden hose ten feet away. That was home for the boy with the bleeding knee.

No wonder he acted so strangely when the workers asked to take him home! Only after seeing the awful place where he lived could they understand his fear and resistance. The child had shown no sense of self-dignity, no sense of self-worth. How could he, with such inadequate housing?

Scripture Selection

Amos 3:15

¹⁵"I will destroy winter houses and summer houses. The houses decorated with ivory will fall in ruins; every large house will be destroyed."

John 14:2-3

²"There are many rooms in my Father's house, and I am going to prepare a place for you. I would not tell you this if it were not so. ³And after I go and prepare a place for you, I will come back and take you to myself, so that you shall be where I am."

Comments on Scripture Selection

Our Scripture selections on the need for shelter come from the prophet Amos and the Gospel of John. Amos was a fiery prophet of Israel in the eighth century BC. Although a so-called "minor prophet," he had a major message about God's concern for justice.

According to Amos, social justice cannot be separated from true religion.

John is usually called the Fourth Gospel because it is placed fourth in the New Testament after the Gospels of Matthew, Mark, and Luke. Some think it was actually written by John, one of the twelve apostles. Its style is very different than that of the first three, and much of its content has no parallels in the other three.

These Scriptures show that God is concerned about housing persons in this world and in the next. Amos 3:15 is very earthy and this-worldly whereas John 14:2-3 is more heavenly and otherworldly.

Amos found some poor persons in his day whose heads had been trampled into the dust of the earth by the rich, some helpless folk who had been sold down the river for silver, and some needy individuals who had been enslaved for a pair of shoes (see Amos 2:6-7).

One of my students found fifteen persons in 1986 living in a one-bedroom apartment in New York City. A newspaper that same year reported the adoption of a fifteen-month-old child in Atlanta, Georgia, who had never been bathed in a bathtub or slept in a bed.

The prophet as God's messenger was telling Israel and us that He did not approve of them or us having two houses when many have no house, or having houses decorated with expensive ivory when many have no house to decorate at all. God wants the poor to be treated justly, and those who have to share generously with the have-nots, according to Amos 5:24, Isaiah 58:6-9, and 1 John 3:17-18.

A favorite religious song in Latin America has a line which says: "I've got nothing in the world but a mansion in the next." That line catches part of the meaning of John 14:2-3. Taken alongside Amos 3:15, John 14:2-3 teaches us that God not only wants us to have decent housing in this life, but He has provided more than adequate housing for His people in the world beyond this one.

Questions to Think About

• If God is so concerned about housing the homeless and decent housing for the poor, why are there three million homeless persons in the United States alone, and many millions living in substandard housing in this country?

• In light of the Scripture selection and of Jeremiah 29:5 and 7, why should I be concerned about housing here as well as in the hereafter?

• Do I see any connection between spending an average of twenty thousand dollars per year to house a nonviolent criminal in prison in America, and the annual amount of approximately $2 billion we are willing to spend on the homeless and housing programs in our nation?

• Should I consider getting personally involved in a housing organization such as Habitat for Humanity (419 West Church Street, Americus, GA 31709), or STEP (Strategies to Elevate People) in Dallas, Texas?

• What resources (skills, money, property, gifts, talents, time,) have I which might be used to meet the housing needs of others such as the injured boy in Pasadena?

• How might I relate what has been said about the need for housing to Psalm 127:1 and Matthew 7:24-27?

Conclusion

Jesus of Nazareth was a homeless person in the first century AD. (see Matt. 8:20). Therefore, He can identify with those who have no place to lay their heads.

If we want persons to respond toward us and others with behavior that is neither strange nor frightening, we shall have to see to it that they have adequate and decent housing.

God wants very much, through His Son and through His people, to meet all the housing needs of all persons in all places throughout all of time and eternity.

6

The Need for Peace

"Every gun that is made, every warship launched, every rocket fired is in a sense a theft from those who hunger and are not fed, those who are cold and not clothed. This is not a way of life at all; it is humanity on a cross of iron." Dwight D. Eisenhower wrote those words nearly three decades ago.

Bread and bombs are rapidly becoming the greatest issues of our world. The three big questions of our time are peace, poverty, and plenty.

The developing world is said to have one soldier for every two-hundred fifty persons, but only one doctor for every thirty-seven hundred. Our world is now spending one million dollars a minute on nuclear weapons. So long as nations spend over $500 billion each year on armaments, the problems of poverty, injustice, and hunger cannot be solved.

An "original child" was born in 1945. The Japanese called the atomic bomb the "original child." They recognized that it was the first of its kind.

Albert Einstein spoke the truth when he said, "The unleashed power of the atom has changed everything except our way of thinking. We shall require a substantially new manner of thinking if mankind is to survive."

The only available data we have on the destructive nature of nuclear war is that from Hiroshima and Nagasaki. On August 6, 1945, a uranium-235 atomic bomb was dropped on Hiroshima. As many as 310,000 civilians and 40,000 soldiers may have been injured. By

December, 1945, it is estimated that 140,000 persons had died from that bomb.

On August 9, 1945, one plutonium-239 atomic bomb was dropped on Nagaski. Approximately 74,000 died from that blast, and another 75,000 were injured. That means 149,000 persons out of 210,000 population were either killed or wounded.

Morton Sontheimer was with the first detachment of Americans to enter Nagasaki after the atom bomb blast. He stood at point zero, the designation of the exact center of the explosion. One of the scientists said to him, "Hey, Captain, you know you're standing on a corpse?"

Sontheimer looked down. His feet were in a circle of fine ash, not thick enough to feel through his boot soles. He was confused and felt embarrassed, as though some sort of apology was called for. As he stepped outside the ashen circle, he resisted a temptation to remove his hat.

There were many such ashen circles in Nagasaki. Later, Sontheimer learned to distinguish the ashes of human beings from those of animals. Further out from point zero other persons were not so fortunate to experience death. Many were disfigured and grotesque, the kind of persons who may be left to repopulate the earth in the event of a nuclear war.

We must stop the arms race or it will stop the human race. Nuclear weapons threaten all of us.

Scripture Selection

Micah 4:3-4

[3]He will settle disputes among the nations,/among the great powers near and far./They will hammer their swords into plows/and their spears into pruning knives./Nations will never again go to war,/never prepare for battle again./[4]Everyone will live in peace/among his own vineyards and fig trees,/and no one will make him afraid./The Lord Almighty has promised this.

John 14:27

²⁷"Peace is what I leave with you; it is my own peace that I give you. I do not give it as the world does. Do not be worried and upset; do not be afraid."

Comments on Scripture Selection

Micah 4:3-4 may be better understood by reading the larger context of 4:1-8. Micah's prophetic vision is of a universal reign of peace tied to the restoration of the nation Israel from Exile (see verses 6 and 7). Here we have one of humankind's first glimpses of a world of justice, law, and peace.

Micah's vision is much like that of Isaiah 2:1-4. Together, these two prophets provide a beautiful picture of God's promised rule. God's rule is one of peace, contentment, and trust.

Verse 3 envisons a theocracy where God Himself would be the earthly ruler of the coming new world. All nations would be merged into a world commonwealth under His shepherdly (see v. 8) rule. The phrase, "He will settle disputes among the nations," means God would be the Judge among them.

The second sentence of verse 3 is what Rolland E. Wolfe called "the first brilliant call for disarmament in the history of the world's thought." Nothing has been said since to surpass the beauty or effectiveness of this classic statement on disarmament. What a splendid vision, the transformation of weapons of warfare into agricultural implements! "Swords into plows/and . . . spears into pruning knives," those words have become picturesque shorthand for world disarmament.

Sentence three of verse 3 restates in straight talk the more symbolical language about plows and pruning knives. The prophet was clearly referring to a future reign of peace. War and preparation for war will be no more. Even though at times this vision may have seemed like an idle dream, the vision will not die; nor should it.

Verse 4 predicts the personal peace and security which the new era will bring to individuals. "Vineyards and fig trees" were symbols of security and peace among the Israelites (see 1 Kings 4:25; Isa. 36:16). "And no one will make him afraid" meant freedom from fear and molestation. Revelation 22:4-5 may be the closest thing in the New Testament to what Micah was saying in verse 4.

John 14:27 points to the role Jesus played in making the ancient and enticing dream of Micah 4:3-4 come true. Many believe that Micah's vision of world peace can only become reality through Jesus Christ, the Prince of peace (Isa. 9:6).

Questions to Think About

• The word *peace* is used at least three different ways in the Bible. There is spiritual peace—peace between God and persons. There is psychological peace—peace within persons. Then there is relational peace—peace among persons. To what kind of peace does Micah 4:3-4 and John 14:27 refer?

• It used to be said that war was waged only between consenting armies. In what way did the dropping of the atomic bombs on Hiroshima and Nagasaki affect that statement?

• In discussions over whether war helps or hurts an economy over the long run, the statement is sometimes made, "Dead persons buy no clothes." Does war ever help a national economy in the long run?

• According to James 4:1-2, what causes wars?

• Does the vision of Micah 4:3-4 excite me? What can I do to turn this dream of peace into reality?

• As the number of nuclear nations grows, some nations which are nuclear "have-nots" are lusting after nuclear weapons. When India exploded her first A-bomb in 1974, Prime Minister Ali Bhutto Of Pakistan swore, "We will eat leaves and grass, even go hungry, but we will have one of our own." How many nations now have their own nuclear weapons?

• Do the visions of the prophet in Micah 4:3-4, or of Jesus in John 14:27, have anything at all in common with the nuclear destruction of Hiroshima and Nagasaki?

Conclusion

A bronze, life-sized statue of Amelia Earhart stands on a three-foot pedestal in her hometown of Atchinson, Kansas. Underneath that statue is an inscription which reads: "Let there be peace on earth, and let it begin with me." Those were the words of the first woman to fly across the Atlantic Ocean. Should we also make them our prayer?

7

The Need for Protection: Part One

Everybody needs protection from something or from someone. Certainly each of us needs protection from natural disasters, plagues, diseases, and pollution.

Protection from lightning may not to be the top priority on your agenda. Yet sixty-eight deaths were blamed on lightning in 1986 in America. That only counts direct hits. It does not include indirect fatalities from such cases as lightning-related fires or falling trees.

Earthquakes continue to take their deadly toll of life and property. Eastern India and Nepal experienced a severe earthquake in 1988 which killed around a thousand persons, injured thousands, and left many thousands homeless. Although that quake lasted only forty-five seconds, its misery and devastation will last for decades. The quake in Soviet Armenia, also in 1988, was even worse.

Floods are an ever-present threat to persons, animals, and certain plants. For example, 1988 floods burst sewage works in Khartoum and contaminated water in the capital city of Sudan. Five thousand cases of disease caught by drinking unclean water were reported. One person had died of cholera in Omdurman, across the Nile River from Khartoum.

Scientists have reported that while the earth's seas have been rising six inches per century, the rate may now increase dramatically. Estimates for rising sea levels range from five to fifteen inches for the year 2025, and from two to seven feet by the year 2100.

While locust plagues may not be very high on your list of dangers, locusts threatened one billion people in 1988. All of Africa, north of the equator, and the entire Middle East as far as India and Pakistan were endangered by swarms of locusts covering a forty-mile square area or more. These three-to-four-inch-long winged creatures devour everything green in their path, wasting crops, trees, and shrubs. They can fly up to 100 miles a day, but they feast at night. We are told that the 1988 antilocust campaign may eventually cost $150 million. This latest outbreak may surpass the 1954 invasion which took more than a decade to wipe out.

History is laden with the heavy toll of plagues. Exodus 10 tells about the terrible plague of locusts in Egypt in the time of Moses. The Black Death of the Middle Ages killed a third of the population of Europe in four years. An influenza epidemic in 1918-19 exterminated more than twenty million persons in a few months. Nowadays AIDS (Acquired Immunity Disease Syndrome) is the new scourge. Already with nearly sixty thousand cases in the United States, there have been thirty-four thousand deaths.

None of us is immune from the threat of natural disasters, deadly diseases, plagues, pollution, and the like. In the Tarheel state where I live, North Carolina's Pamlico River is rapidly becoming unfit for fish and other sea life. This is not from the dumping of illegal chemicals, like kepone which so damaged the James River in Virginia. Instead, our officials tells us the pollution is caused by legal discharges.

Scripture Selection

Psalms 146:1-10

[1]Praise the Lord!/Praise the Lord, my soul!/[2]I will praise him as long as I live;/I will sing to my God all my life./[3]Don't put your trust in human leaders;/no human being can save you./[4]When they die, they return to the dust;/on that day all their plans come to an end./ [5]Happy is the man who has the/God of Jacob to help him/and who depends on the Lord his God,/[6]the Creator of heaven, earth, and sea,/and all that is in them./He always keeps his promises;/[7]he judges in favor of the oppressed/and gives food to the hungry./The Lord sets prisoners free/[8]and gives sight to the blind./He lifts those who have fallen;/he loves his righteous people./[9]He protects the strangers who live in our land;/he helps widows and orphans,/but ruins the plans of the wicked./[10]The Lord is king forever./Your God, O Zion, will reign for all time./Praise the Lord!

Matthew 8:23-27

[23]Jesus got into a boat, and his disciples went with him. [24]Suddenly a fierce storm hit the lake, and the boat was in danger of sinking. But Jesus was asleep. [25]The disciples went to him and woke him up. "Save us, Lord!" they said. "We are about to die!"

[26]"Why are you so frightened?" Jesus answered. "What little faith you have!" Then he got up and ordered the winds and the waves to stop, and there was a great calm.

[27]Everyone was amazed. "What kind of man is this?" they said. "Even the winds and the waves obey him!"

Comments on Scripture Selection

Please notice that Psalm 146 is the first of five psalms which begin with the words, "Praise the Lord!" Psalms 146 through 150 are a collection of five hallelujah songs in the Hebrew songbook. These five psalms are congregational hymns of praise. Psalm 146, however, is the personal testimony of the psalmist to the goodness of God. This song has the ring of real experience behind it. The psalmist might have gone through some personal crisis in which he had learned that human leaders are a poor source of hope and help, as over against the Creator of all things.

Verses 1 and 2 are a vow to praise God so long as the psalmist lived. Verses 3 and 4 warn against putting ultimate trust in human leaders. Verses 5-7 are a pronouncement of happiness on those who depend on God. Those who put their trust in God will never be disappointed because of His power, faithfulness, and character (see vv. 6-7).

Like the prophets of Israel, the psalmist here, as elsewhere (see Pss. 10; 15; 24; 37; 72; 94; 103), sounds a social note. God is concerned about the welfare of the oppressed, the hungry, prisoners, the blind, the fallen, widows, and orphans (see vv. 7-9). The Lord's rule, unlike all earthly rulers, will never come to an end (v. 10).

Matthew 8:23-27 was a miracle over nature performed by Jesus Christ, the Lord over winds and waves and over all. The New Testament identifies Jesus as "the one through whom God created the universe" (Heb. 1:2; see also John 1:3). If we will compare Psalm 146:5-6 and verse 10 with Matthew 8:26-27, we may see that both Scriptures teach the Lordship of God over all—including nature and history. Those who look to God for their salvation, whether that salvation be physical deliverance or spiritual rescue, need not be frightened. Both of the Scripture selections teach that God and God alone is our Savior.

Questions to Think About

• Can I identify some experience of crisis in my life journey which enables me to praise the Lord as long as I live (see Ps. 146:2)?

• Am I afraid of natural disasters, plagues, dread diseases, and pollution because of a wholesome and intelligent regard for such dangers or because of what Jesus called "little faith" (see Matt. 8:26)?

• If I believe God created the physical universe and everything in it, why can't I also believe that God is Lord over all physical matter, and that this world is essentially a friendly place?

• How can I relate what is written in Colossians 1:16-17 to what I know about the destructive forces of nature and disease?

• What does human stewardship over God's creation (see Ps. 8:6-8) have to do with the pollution of our rivers and seas?

• What obligations do I have to protect myself and my neighbors from natural disasters, plagues, diseases, and pollution?

Conclusion

The Hebrew psalmist wrote of God in Psalms 4:1, "When I was in trouble, you helped me." The Revised Standard Version put it like this: "Thou hast given me room when I was in distress." We might even translate the verse to read: "Thou hast enlarged me when I was in distress." If, as the psalmist said, God "always keeps his promises" (Ps. 146:6), then we can count on Him to help us—to give us room, to enlarge us, in the tough times and in the tight places of our life's journey. Indeed, if we have a large enough faith, He might even enable us, like Jesus, to sleep in a small boat through a fierce storm (see Matt. 8:24).

8

The Need for Protection: Part Two

MacKenzie Phillips at the age of fourteen starred in *American Graffiti*. Yet she was dropped from the television show "One Day at a Time" because cocaine reduced her five-foot-seven-inch body to 90 pounds, and she could not function.

John Phillips, MacKenzie's father, was the prime mover of the folk-rock group The Mamas and the Papas. Both father and daughter say their journey into oblivion started with marijuana. They contend adamantly that it should not be legalized.

John Phillips dropped from 210 pounds to 140 pounds. When his daughter turned to him for help, her father was shooting up on heroin as often as every fifteen minutes. "I almost lost my leg from gangrene," he said. "By that time," he continued, "I was too far gone to help her with her problem. Once you become addicted to narcotics, it's a very strange thing, but family doesn't seem to matter. Position, integrity, your morals—the whole thing crumbles right beneath you."

Is there any question that persons need protection from illegal drugs that lay such waste to human beings? Illegal trafficking in drugs has become a major concern to governments, families, and individuals. Violence, corruption, and organized crime keep close company with drug smuggling.

What shall we say of alcoholic beverages? Alcohol really witnesses against itself. It causes 60 percent of teenage deaths on the highway and 50 percent of all highway deaths. One study showed that 50 percent of pedestrians killed in accidents had been drinking.

We need protection from drinking and drunk drivers, and from a whole lot of other kinds of crime and criminals to boot. In 1987 in Los Angeles, California, during a six-week period there were at least twenty hot-tempered highway shootings. Three persons died, and four others were wounded, one critically. Apparently some folk thought that they could go out on the freeways and play cowboys with cars and guns. Talk of gunplay filled local news broadcasts. Auto-glass installers reported increased requests for bulletproof windows.

You and I live in a world where there is some danger. Not even the president of the United States is completely safe. When President Ronald Reagan was shot in 1981, Mrs. Reagan said she became "obsessed with his safety."

Scripture Selection

Psalms 27:1-3

[1]The Lord is my light and my salvation;/I will fear no one./The Lord protects me from all danger;/I will never be afraid./[2]When evil

men attack me and try to kill me,/they stumble and fall./[3]Even if a whole army surrounds me,/I will not be afraid;/even if enemies attack me, I will still trust in God.

Romans 8:35-39

[35]Who, then, can separate us from the love of Christ? Can trouble do it, or hardship or persecution or hunger or poverty, or danger or death? [36]As the scripture says,/"For your sake we are in danger of death at all times;/we are treated like sheep that are going to be slaughtered."/[37]No, in all these things we have complete victory through him who loved us! [38]For I am certain that nothing can separate us from his love: neither death nor life, neither angels nor other heavenly rulers or powers, neither the present nor the future, [39]neither the world above nor the world below—there is nothing in all creation that will ever be able to separate us from the love of God which is ours through Christ Jesus our Lord.

Comments on Scripture Selection

One good way to get at the meaning of Psalm 27:1-3 would be to read all fourteen verses of the psalm. Note how it falls into two divisions, the first going through verse 6, and the second verses 7-14. The major thread which holds the two parts together is their common element of trust in God in the face of assaults from enemies. God is spoken of in the third person in verses 1-6, but in the second person in verses 7-14. Things seem to be going exceedingly well for the psalmist in part one, whereas in part two things seem to be going exceedingly ill.

Nevertheless, in spite of the two contrasting moods expressed in the psalm, the constancy of God's protective care fueled the psalmist's hope for eventual deliverance. He concluded, "I know that I will live to see/the Lord's goodness in this present life" (Ps. 27:13).

Verse 1 proclaims the fullness of the psalmist's trust in the Lord. The certainty of these affirmations about God being his helper may relect some bitter personal trials and troubles through which the psalmist had passed.

"The Lord is my light" meant the Lord was his source of joy (Ps. 97:11), prosperity, (Job 29:3), and life (Ps. 36:9). It also meant the light of leadership. In other words, God showed the psalmist the right paths in which to go. "My salvation" was another way of saying "My light." This first verse, along with all of verses 1-6, was often used by Scottish Christians in celebrating the death of Christ. The opening line of their hymn said, "The Lord's my light and saving health."

"The Lord protects me from all danger" is translated "the strength of my life" in the King James Version, and "the stronghold of my life" in the Revised Standard Version. The idea which the psalmist wished to convey was that the Lord was his refuge in times of danger. With such resources on his side, he could assert with confidence, "I will fear no one", and "I will never be afraid."

Compare verse 2 with verse 12 of Psalm 27. The verse pictured warlike combat. In fact, the original Hebrew for this verse indicates that the evil men who sought to kill the psalmist were emphatically his enemies. They attacked him violently and without mercy.

"They stumble and fall" indicates that what the evildoers intended to do to the psalmist would become their fate. Verse 3 is a vigorous summary and restatement of the firm confidence expressed in verses 1 and 2.

Romans 8:35-39 teaches us that those who have the kind of trust in the Lord that the psalmist expressed in Psalm 27:1-3 can absolutely count on God to never permit anything to separate them from the love which He has shown for the world in Jesus Christ (see Rom. 5:1-11; John 3:16). Verse 36 is a quotation from Psalms 44:22.

Questions to Think About

• How can I account for the two different moods expressed by the psalmist in Psalm 27?

• Are things going exceedingly well for me right now or exceedingly ill?

• What kind of protection do I need most right now? Is it from drugs (illegal or legal)? Is it from alcohol abuse? Is it from crime or criminals? Is it from some vehement enemy?

• Do I know someone personally and up close who has become a victim of drugs, alcohol, or crime?

• What *can* I do to protect the John and MacKenzie Phillipses of my world? What *should* I do?

• As I review the long list of things in Romans 8:35-39 which may seek to separate me from the love of God, which one of them is my greatest enemy?

Conclusion

Psalms 36:9 says of God, "Because of your light we see the light." The light of God means joy, prosperity, life, and leadership. What light have I gained from this study which may give me the protection I need, and which may make me a better protector of my neighbors?

9

The Need for Work

The late Louis L'Amour, while in his late seventies after writing ninety-five books, said: "There's so much I want to know, so many stories I have left to tell." When L'Amour died at the age of eighty, all 101 of his books were in print with almost two-hundred million copies in circulation. He enjoyed his work so much that he wrote five pages every day, including Sundays and holidays.

Although L'Amour didn't start writing until he was about forty-five years old, this former longshoreman, lumberjack, elephant handler, fruit picker, and officer on a tank destroyer in World War II was the first novelist to be awarded a congressional gold medal. Moreover, the millions who have bought and read his books testify to the quality of his workmanship.

Now set alongside the distinguished work of L'Amour the faithful work of a little-known Christian social worker, and see if you can find a story within her story. Sister Mary Teresa Floyd, a nun in the Sisters of the Good Shepherd order, has spent most of her twenty-five-year career working with teenage delinquents. For the past five years Sister Teresa has been director of volunteers at the North Carolina Correctional Center for Women. She became interested in prison work because she says jails were first set up by churches as a humane alternative to the way criminals were usually treated. Torture or execution were common. However, the irony is that now jails and prisons have "turned out to be so inhumane."

Referring to the prisoners with whom she worked, Sister Teresa said, "Their lives are the most total waste of humanity I've ever seen." Especially does she see that waste in the "long-termers," those who serve sentences of twenty years or more. Their problems are: mental anguish, isolation, lack of privacy, having to ask for everything, losing their ability to make a choice, and depression. As one inmate stated, "The emotional level in here is probably three times as high as anywhere else."

Sister Teresa believes that a better solution than long-term confinement to prison should be found for the nonviolent and repentant prisoners. "I'm not a do-gooder," she says. "I believe people should be responsible for what they do. But I also believe society should be responsible." This realistic Christian social worker reminds us that when you lock persons out of your society, they're going to be scarred by prison. When they get out and come back into society, some of them are going to be bitter.

Whether we are happily employed in some meaningful occupation surely makes a big difference in us and in our world, doesn't it? Yet we are living in a day when one newspaper ad for a "handyman" elicited over three-hundred calls. The lady who placed that ad said she was dumbfounded by the avalanche of callers, especially by the number of college-educated and overqualified applicants.

Earlier this decade it was reported that one British father placed a newspaper advertisement offering a forty-five-hundred-dollar reward to any firm that would hire his son as an electrician's apprentice. That same report said 40 percent of the jobless persons in the European Common Market were less than twenty-five years of age.

Unemployment runs as high as 50 percent in the Dominican Republic. One man had not been able to find work for over two years. Unemployed persons are more than a curve on some economic chart. They are not mere masses of protoplasm.

Scripture Selection

Exodus 20:8-11

[8]"Observe the Sabbath and keep it holy. [9]You have six days in which to do your work, [10]but the seventh day is a day of rest dedicated to me. On that day no one is to work—neither you, your children, your slaves, your animals, nor the foreigners who live in your country. [11]In six days I, the Lord, made the earth, the sky, the seas, and everything in them, but on the seventh day I rested. That is why I, the Lord, blessed the Sabbath and made it holy."

2 Thessalonians 3:6-13

[6]Our brothers, we command you in the name of our Lord Jesus Christ to keep away from all brothers who are living a lazy life and who do not follow the instructions that we gave them.

You yourselves know very well that you should do just what we did. We were not lazy when we were with you. [8]We did not accept anyone's support without paying for it. Instead, we worked and toiled; we kept working day and night so as not to be an expense to any of you. [9]We did this, not because we do not have the right to demand our support; we did it to be an example for you to follow. [10]While we were with you, we used to tell you, "Whoever refuses to work is not allowed to eat."

[11]We say this because we hear that there are some people among you who live lazy lives and who do nothing except meddle in other people's business. [12]In the name of the Lord Jesus Christ we com-

mand these people and warn them to lead orderly lives and work to
earn their own living.

¹³But you, brothers, must not become tired of doing good.

Comments on Scripture Selection

Exodus 20:8-11 is the fourth of the Ten Commandments which
God gave to the nation Israel through his servant Moses. Behind this
ancient law of the Sabbath is some infinite wisdom about the rhythm
of work and rest. Work and worship are integral to each other.

God, the Master Worker, set a perfect example for us to follow in
His creation of the universe (see v. 11; and Gen. 2:1-3). Genesis
1:1-31 gives a detailed account of God's creative work referred to in
Exodus 20:11.

Second Thessalonians 3:6-13 should probably be understood
against the background of some Thessalonian Christians' misunder-
standing of the second coming of Christ (see especially 2 Thess.
2:1-12). Some of them might have thought the Lord's coming was so
close there was no point in working. Others among them may have
been so spiritually minded that they let others work to provide for
their needs while they gave themselves to heavenly things. Whatever
the reason for their idleness, Paul counseled them all to work, and
to work in accordance with the example which he and his fellow
workers had shown while in Thessalonica.

Daily work is important, even if it happens to be unspectacular or
humdrum. Proper Christian teaching is that the servants of Christ are
to work hard and to do their work well. These words from Paul sound
much like Proverbs 6:6-11.

Questions to Think About

• Do I enjoy my work as Louis L'Amour enjoyed his, and if not,
why?

• What is the story within the story of Sister Mary Teresa Floyd?
Why do many prisoners have no meaningful work to do?

• Does God want everybody who can work to have a decent job?

• What do I think God may be saying to the "workaholic" in Exodus 20:8-11?

• Based on my experience and observation, do I think persons today are more like Louis L'Amour or those in Thessalonica "who live lazy lives and who do nothing except meddle in other people's business" (2 Thess. 3:11)?

• Exodus 20:8-11 reveals God as the Master Worker (see also Gen. 1:1-31). What can I learn about work from this perfect example.

• Paul in 2 Thessalonians 3:7-10 lifts up himself and his co-workers as example workers for the Thessalonians. What can I learn about work from this example?

Conclusion

My experience and observation tell me that most persons want worthwhile work. Only a tiny minority are like the lazy sluggards of Proverbs 6:6-11.

Our modern technological cultures are, of course, vastly different than those of Israel and the early church. Nevertheless, what is said about work in the Bible continues to be true and can be translated into our settings. We can take comfort in the fact that God knows our need for meaningful work and cares about our economic well-being.

10

The Need for Money

Opulence and greed are alive and well on planet Earth. *The Wall Street Journal* reported some poor and handicapped persons were evicted from their homes and apartments by landlords in Knoxville,

Tennessee, during the 1982 World's Fair. They were not always evicted directly, but some were put out subtly by having their rent raised. One apartment owner raised his rent from $285 to $385 a month. When his apartments were vacant, he could charge $144 per day during the duration of the fair. When asked how he got up to this act, the man said; "I'm a Christian, and I prayed before I did this."

It appears that none of us is exempt from possible greed for money, and it is certain that each of us needs money. Even our children and youth quickly learn about money. A group of eighth graders in Springfield, Illinois, recently cooked up some new adages about money which may one day become old. Here is a sampling:

"Currency is the source of corruption."
"Money is the answer to all bills."
"A rolling stone gathers no money until it is a rock star."

One of the biggest lessons all of us soon learn about money is the wide gap between the "haves" and "the have-nots."

Photographer Margaret Bourke-White, in her work for *Life* magazine, doggedly pursued photos around the world. One of her most striking pictures made in 1937 contrasted the plight of black Louisville, Kentucky, flood victims with a billboard showing a happy and prosperous white family. The billboard showed a family of four well-dressed, prosperous-looking, smiling members along with their family dog driving along in a beautiful automobile. In big bold letters all the way across the top of the billboard were the words: World's Highest Standard of Living. Over to the side of the automobile in smaller print were the words: There's No Way Like the American Way. Juxtaposed against the backdrop of that giant billboard was a line of sixteen or more sad-looking blacks waiting in line with bags and baskets for handouts of food. What an unforgettable contrast between the haves and the have-nots! And the gap between them continues to widen.

Scripture Selection

Isaiah 55:1-2

[1]The LORD says,/"Come, everyone who is thirsty—/here is wa-ter!/Come, you that have no money—/buy grain and eat!/Come! Buy wine and milk—/it will cost you nothing!/[2]Why spend money on what does not satisfy?/Why spend your wages and still be hungry?/Listen to me and do what I say,/and you will enjoy the best food of all."

Matthew 6:24-34

[24]"No one can be a slave of two masters; he will hate one and love the other; he will be loyal to one and despise the other. You cannot serve both God and money.

[25]"This is why I tell you: do not be worried about the food and drink you need in order to stay alive, or about clothes for your body. After all, isn't life worth more than food? And isn't the body worth more than clothes? [26]Look at the birds flying around: they do not plant seeds, gather a harvest and put it in barns; yet your Father in heaven takes care of them! Aren't you worth much more than birds? [27]Can any of you live a bit longer by worrying about it?

[28]"And why worry about clothes? Look how the wild flowers grow: they do not work or make clothes for themselves. [29]But I tell you not even King Solomon with all his wealth had clothes as beautiful as one of these flowers. [30]It is God who clothes the wild grass— grass that is here today and gone tomorrow, burned up in the oven. Won't he be all the more sure to clothe you? What little faith you have!

[31]"So do not start worrying: 'Where will my food come from? or my drink? or my clothes?' [32](These are the things the pagans are always concerned about.) Your Father in heaven knows that you need all these things. [33]Instead, be concerned above everything else with the Kingdom of God and with what he requires of you, and he will provide you with all these other things. [34]So do not worry about

tomorrow; it will have enough worries of its own. There is no need to add to the troubles each day brings.

Comments on Scripture Selection

The setting for the great invitation of Isaiah 55:1-2 is Babylon where the people of Israel were in exile because of their sins. God, through His prophet, invited His exiled people to come to Him for forgiveness and a new exodus into their Promised Land (see Isa. 55:12). In order to get a feel for Isaiah's message, you may want to read all of chapter 55.

Water, grain, wine, and milk were the symbols of new life with God. These gifts were God's blessings bestowed upon those who subjected themselves to His rule. The eating and drinking point to a celebration of new life.

Verse 2 makes it clear that "the best food" is spiritual, that is, that only God Himself could fill what H. G. Wells called the "God-shaped blank" in persons' lives (see Pss. 36:8; 63:5).

The words *you will enjoy the best food of all* are perhaps more literally translated by the King James Version: "Let your soul delight itself in fatness." The soul in Hebrew psychology was the seat of the appetite. What the prophet wished to convey was that true prosperity comes from God. Perhaps we should find it instructive that the new life which God offers includes material welfare and physical well-being as well as spiritual blessings.

Water, like the other three items of grain, wine, and milk, had to be purchased in Oriental cities. These items boiled down to drink and food, the necessities of life. Yet God offers them free of charge to "everyone," including those "that have no money."

Matthew 6:24-34 are the words of Jesus. They are a part of His larger Sermon on the Mount (see Matt. 5:1 through 7:29) and address the subject of God and possessions. Verse 24 is the peg around which verses 25-34 hang and, especially, the statement, "You cannot serve both God and money." The word *money* used here meant property or riches.

The body was not unimportant to Jesus. He recognized that the body needed food, drink, and clothes (see Matt. 6:25-32). Verse 32 is a kind of summary word on bodily needs, "Your Father in heaven knows that you need all these things." But Jesus called persons to "be concerned above everything else" with God and His will (v. 33). He made the point that God who feeds the birds (v. 26), and clothes the wild flowers and grass (vv. 28-30), can all the more sure be counted on to help us with our physical and material needs.

Questions to think About

• Based on my understanding of Isaiah 55:1-2 and Matthew 6:24-34, do they teach that money itself is evil? How does my answer square with 1 Timothy 6:10?

• Am I now a victim of my own greed or of someone else's greed?

• If I had to identify myself with either "the haves" or "the have-nots" of the world, with which group would I place myself?

• Is there any scriptural support in either Isaiah 55:1-2 or in Matthew 6:24-34 for the adage: "Money is the answer to all bills"?

• In the two biblical passages cited above, what can I find which teaches that God is concerned about physical and material needs as well as spiritual needs?

• There is a quotation which goes like this: "Out of money, out of work, and out of favor." How do Isaiah 55:1-2 and Matthew 6:24-34 contradict that quotation?

Conclusion

In 1979 Vu Thuy (pronounced *voo twee*) escaped Vietnam in a raft with eighty other refugees. Vu won the first Twenty-first Century Woman Award in 1987 for her work with Vietnamese boat people in San Diego. On receiving the award, the brown-eyed five-foot-one-inch Vu, age thirty-seven, said: "I owe my life to so many mysterious things. I feel a debt that I have to pay for all people."

If, like Vu Thuy, you and I begin to see ourselves as debtors to God and to others, we shall have already begun to receive and to share the prosperity which He freely offers us all (see Isa. 55:1-2).

PART III
LOVE AND RELATIONAL NEEDS

11

The Need for Love

Medical doctor Bernie S. Siegel, in his book *Love, Medicine, and Miracles,* wrote about a secretary named Sherry. Sherry, as a child, felt unloved by her stepmother. As a teenager, she formed a strong attachment to one of her teachers. In the school gym one day, Sherry mentioned to some of her friends that she loved Mrs. Johnson. Some of the students told the teacher, "Sherry loves you," whereupon Mrs. Johnson called Sherry into her office.

"Sherry, do you love me from near or far?" asked her teacher. Not knowing what Mrs. Johnson was talking about, Sherry answered, "From near."

The teacher called Sherry's stepmother and told her that Sherry was a lesbian. The stepmother confronted Sherry with the information when she returned home from school that day. Much later, Sherry told Dr. Siegel, "I didn't know what 'lesbian' meant, but I got the message that love gets you in trouble, and I decided to stop loving."

Sherry lost her friends. She became lonely and so desperate that she "would get dressed and walk the streets hoping people would look out their windows and wave at me." Finally, Sherry got married, but she had difficulty believing in her husband's love. Over and over, Sherry kept asking her husband if he loved her. After having six children, she developed cervical cancer. When she first came to Dr. Siegel, Sherry told him, "I know if I hadn't developed cancer he would have left me."

Sherry did open her heart to love. She made a stand against her illness. But she never fully recovered from the lack of real love in her formative years.

While the story of Sherry is only one flesh-and-blood example of the need for love, does it not point us to the universal need of all persons to be loved and to love?

Businessman Owen Cooper of Yazoo City, Mississippi, died at the age of seventy-eight in 1986. Toward the end of his life, Cooper wrote a poem entitled: "If I Had My Life to Live Over." The first two stanzas of that poem say:

> If I had my life to live over,
>   I would love more.
> I would especially love others more.
> I would let this love express itself in
>   a concern for my neighbors,
>   my friends, and all with whom I came in contact.
>
> I would try to let love permeate me,
>   overcome me, overwhelm me, and direct me.
> I would love the unlovely, the unwanted,
>   the unknown, and the unloved.

Scripture Selection

Psalms 136:26

26Give thanks to the God of heaven;/his love is eternal.

1 Corinthians 13:1-13

1I may be able to speak the languages of men and even of angels, but if I have no love, my speech is no more than a noisy gong or a clanging bell. 2I may have the gift of inspired preaching; I may have all knowledge and understand all secrets; I may have all the faith needed to move mountains—but if I have no love, I am nothing. 3I may give away everything I have, and even give up my body to be burned—but if I have no love, this does me no good.

4Love is patient and kind; it is not jealous or conceited or proud; 5love is not ill-mannered or selfish or irritable; love does not keep a record of wrongs; [6]love is not happy with evil, but is happy with the truth. [7]Love never gives up; and its faith, hope, and patience never fail.

[8]Love is eternal. There are inspired messages, but they are temporary; there are gifts of speaking in strange tongues, but they will cease; there is knowledge, but it will pass. [9]For our gifts of knowledge and of inspired messages are only partial; [10]but when what is perfect comes, then what is partial will disappear.

[11]When I was a child, my speech, feelings, and thinking were all those of a child; now that I am a man, I have no more use for childish ways. [12]What we see now is like a dim image in a mirror; then we shall see face-to-face. What I know now is only partial; then it will be complete—as complete as God's knowledge of me.

[13]Meanwhile these three remain: faith, hope, and love; and the greatest of these is love.

Comments on Scripture Selection

Psalm 136:26 repeats the opening theme (see vv. 1-3) of this Hebrew hymn of thanksgiving for the goodness and love of God. Twenty-six times in this psalm the words *his love is eternal* are repeated. The Hebrew word translated "love" in *The Good News Bible* is translated "mercy" in the King James Version and "steadfast love" in the Revised Standard Version. It is the word for God's covenant love in the Old Testament and implies kindness, fidelity, and loyalty.

I call Psalm 136 "The Steadfast Love Psalm." The psalm calls us to thank God for His love expressed in the creation of all (vv. 4-9), in Israel's history (vv. 10-22), and in His providential care over His people and all flesh (vv. 23-25). Verse 26 concludes the hymn with words which sum up everything said in verses 1-25.

First Corinthians 13 is Paul's great love hymn in which he sang the praises of love, which Henry Drummond called "the greatest thing in the world." The Greek word used here for "love" is *agape*. These thirteen verses provide a well-rounded definition of love.

Verses 1-3 tell about the desirability of love by pointing to its preeminence over other spiritual gifts and by contrasting love with other skills. The bottom line in this entire paragraph is: whatever else I may have, "if I have no love, I am nothing" (v. 2).

Verses 4-7 give a description of love by telling what its characteristics are, and by focusing it through a prism which reveals all of its rainbow colors. Paul's description of love sounds like his description of Jesus Christ in Philippians 2:5-8 (see also Eph. 4:32 through 5:2).

Verses 8-13 focus on the durability of love by showing its permanence over everything else, and by revealing love's continuation into the time when "we shall see face-to-face" (v. 12). All other gifts are partial and will pass away, but "Love is eternal" (v. 8).

Questions to Think About

• If I had my life to live over, would I love more as Owen Cooper said he would?

• Based on what Scripture says in Psalms 136:26 and in 1 Corinthians 13:8, do I now believe God loves me with a love that will never let go? And when I compare John 3:16 with these verses, should I believe that God loves every person in the world with an eternal love?

• Sherry's teacher, Mrs. Johnson, mistakenly identified Sherry's love for her with sexual love. Do I know anyone who has made the same mistake?

• One has written, "Love is a consistant attitude of personal humility and devotion to the good of others." How does that definition square with my understanding of what is meant by love in Psalm 136 and 1 Corinthians 13?

• How does the example of Sherry show both the need to be loved and the need to love?

• If Sherry had been loved with the kind of love described in 1 Corinthians 13:4-7, what difference do I think might have been made in her story?

• According to the comments on the Scripture selection above, Paul's description of love in 1 Corinthians 13:4-7 sounds like his description elsewhere of whom?

Conclusion

You might have seen that unusual television commercial about helping lepers. The first picture showed a helper actually touching a victim of leprosy. A voice said, "I wouldn't do that for a million dollars." Then, the helper spoke, "Neither would I." Finally, silently trailed across the screen were the words of Paul from 2 Corinthians 5:14, "We are ruled by the love of Christ."

Mother Teresa stated the same truth in these words: "I try to give to the poor people for love what the rich could get for money. No, I wouldn't touch a leper for a thousand pounds; yet I willingly cure him for the love of God."

12

The Need to Belong

John, a young man of about twenty-three, showed up at Charlie's Boston-suburb restaurant one cold day in February, about two years ago. He didn't come to the front door near the cashier's cage but to the kitchen door. John was looking for a job—not a particular job but just any job.

According to Charlie, the fat and friendly owner of this relaxed restaurant, John was half frozen to death and a lot skinnier than he is now. He had no hat, no mittens, and a thin jacket that was ready for the garbage dump. Shivering, he reminded Charlie of a dog that had been kicked around so long it's half ready to tuck its tail and run. Charlie got him into the kitchen to warm up and gave him a plate of ham and eggs. John never looked up. He didn't say a word but just devoured the food like he was starved to death.

Charlie gave John a job, taught him how to clear and set tables, how to cook and carry trays of silver, china, and glassware to the kitchen dishwasher. "John can't seem to do some things that other people can," said Charlie, "but I didn't hesitate to hire him because nobody that works here is ever going to give him a hard time."

John is still like a windblown leaf. Once he told Charlie that he had never received a letter or had a phone call in his life. Even now, two years later, none of the other restaurant workers knows where he came from, whether he ever went to school or has parents, brothers, or sisters. What they do know about John is that he is hungry to relate to people, and especially to the restaurant staff. They also know some of the devices he has created to conceal his differences from those whom he considers his friends.

John doesn't tell jokes even if he could remember them, which he cannot. Nor does he understand jokes or know why they are funny. Yet he listens to his comrades as they tell jokes. He has even learned to imitate the expressions on his friends' faces as they anticipate the joke being told. By watching his friends laugh, he enjoys laughing with them, even if he can't comprehend why they are laughing.

When the restaurant staff started a softball team, John bought a new glove as though he intended to be on the softball team. Each day the team is scheduled to play, he brings his glove to work. But he never shows up for the games or for practice. Always he says he's sorry and makes some excuse. The restaurant owner knows that John can't learn to play softball and could not remember how if he did learn.

The fellows who work at Charlie's all have girl friends or wives. Some have children. Their kitchen talk is much about their girls, wives, children, families, domestic problems, and the good and bad aspects of these relationships. During the past two years John has met a girl named Mildred, courted her, gotten engaged, married, received a raise because of his marriage, expected a baby, and had his wife to die from cancer. The wedding was out of town, so was the funeral. Therefore, John's friends never got to meet Mildred.

Mildred, of course, existed only in John's mind. "So now John is like everybody else here," said Charlie. "He knows what it's like to be married and have your ups and downs; he can say he, too, has been there." Charlie continued, "What's important is that John can regard himself as a man who has lived like other men, and that makes him happy."

Scripture Selection

Exodus 19:3-8

The Lord called to him from the mountain and told him to say to the Israelites, Jacob's descendants: 4"You saw what I, the Lord, did to the Egyptians and how I carried you as an eagle carries her young on her wings, and brought you here to me. 5Now, if you will obey me and keep my covenant, you will be my own people. The whole earth is mine, but you will be my chosen people, 6a people dedicated to me alone, and you will serve me as priests." 7So Moses went down and called the leaders of the people together and told them everything that the Lord had commanded him. 8Then all the people answered together, "We will do everything that the Lord has said," and Moses reported this to the Lord.

1 Peter 2:9-10

9But you are a chosen race, the King's priests, the holy nation, God's own people, chosen to proclaim the wonderful acts of God, who called you out of darkness into his own marvelous light. 10At one time you were not God's people, but now you are his people; at one time you did not know God's mercy, but now you have received his mercy.

Comments on Scripture Selection

The selection from Exodus 19:3-8 picks up in the middle of verse 3 because that's the way *The Good News Bible* prints the passage. Bible students sometime refer to these verses as the eagle-wings passage (see v. 4). Eagles frequently push young eaglets out of their nests in order to teach them to fly. The mother eagle, on the first attempts of her young, swoops underneath, gathers them to safety and carries them on her strong wings. That's like what God did in rescuing the nation Israel from Egypt.

Exodus 19:5 uses the word *covenant* to describe the relationship between God and Israel. *Berith* was the Hebrew word for *covenant,* a common term for an agreement or a contract. From Mount Sinai onward, covenant became the designation for that special relationship established between God and Israel as a response to God's salvation in the Exodus events. Note that the Ten Commandments in Exodus 20:2 begin with the acknowledgment, "I am the Lord your God who brought you out of Egypt, where you were slaves."

God had delivered the Israelites in the Exodus (see v. 4), but here at Mount Sinai (see Ex. 19:2) the Hebrews became a people (see vv. 5-6). At Sinai, Israel became a community of faith and chose to harness her future to divine power in covenant obedience. "We will do everything that the Lord has said" (v. 8). Old Testament scholar Bruce C. Birch summed it up this way: "Israel was liberated *from* oppression and suffering but was liberated *for* community and mutual responsibility" (see Lev. 19:17-18).

First Peter 2:9-10 applies the same titles of privilege and responsibility used in Exodus 19:5-6 to the Christian church. The first part of verse 9 describes the church as "the chosen race, the King's priests, the holy nation, God's own people." Part two of verse 9 spells out the mission of the community of Christ. Verse 10 is a kind of postscript on how the church came to be God's people. It was through no merit of her own but solely by the mercy of God.

According to these words in 1 Peter 2, God's promise to Israel in Exodus 19:5-6 is fulfilled by the church, the ideal Israel. Through Christ and the New Covenant which He established by His death and resurrection, the church has become the Israel of God. A comparison of 1 Peter 2:10 with Hosea 2:23 (see also Hos. 1:6-8) will show that Peter taught Hosea's prophecy concerning Loruhamah and Loammi (KJV) was fulfilled when God brought His new community of the church into being.

Questions to Think About

• In Exodus 19:3-8, what provision did God make for Israel's need to belong to Him and to one another?

• According to 1 Peter 2:9-10, what provision has God made for all persons to belong to Him and to one another?

• Was God's election of Israel or of the church intended to *exclude* or to *include* persons like John?

• Do I know any person who, like John, has never received a letter or had a phone call in his or her life?

• If my need to belong has been met, what am I doing to reach out to the Johns of the world to help them feel that they belong?

• With whom do I identify most in that suburban Boston restaurant, John or Charlie?

• Have I taken any time lately to thank God for the Charlies of the world? When did I last speak a word of appreciation or encouragement to some Charlie in my sphere of influence?

Conclusion

God created persons for community, not for loneliness, isolation, or alienation. He wants us—the Johns and Charlies and everybody else—to belong to Him and to one another. That's the reason He made a contract with Israel in Exodus 19 and with the church in 1 Peter 2.

13

The Need for Family

One day as I was out for a walk I passed a house in my neighborhood that had pink-and-blue balloons strung across the front porch. From the nearby trees hung long streamers of blue toilet tissue, and a huge blue ribbon adorned the mailbox. On the front lawn was a crude cardboard sign which had obviously been made by the children of the family. It read:

> Congratulations Mom and Dad
> It's a Boy!

It gave me a wonderful feeling to see what a welcome this new addition was getting as he became a member of that family.

This kind of welcome didn't just happen. Much preparation had been made ahead of time. In the first place, the children had to feel pretty secure with themselves to extend such a welcome. I imagine that the mother and father had begun preparing their children for the new baby's arrival about seven or eight months before. Most likely this began shortly after being told that their mother was expecting a baby.

After each visit to the obstetrician, can't you imagine the mother telling her children about how large the baby must be at that time? She probably began the bonding early as she placed their little hands on her stomach, so they could feel their little brother or sister move. Or perhaps she had them place their ears up to her stomach to see if they could hear the baby.

A little later on, they could have gone on a hospital tour to see where their mother would go when the baby was born. Perhaps the nurse would even show them a special room where their father would bring them to visit their mother and the baby.

I can see in my mind's eye a lot of talk in that family about the new addition, what his or her name would be, how the children would be the baby's big brothers and sisters, and how dependent it would be on everyone for everything. There would be more discussion as they began getting the nursery ready, purchasing furniture, clothing, and other necessary items.

Throw your mental switch and look with me now at a very different story. The setting is Philadelphia, the city of brotherly love. A father of four children is a textbook alcoholic who beat his children, wrecked his house, and humiliated his family in front of friends. This man's own son said, "I hated my father for the first twenty years of my life."

When the son was five, his father borrowed twenty dollars from the parish priest; then he took the boy to the local beer hall where for the next three hours they rehearsed the amount of money—fifteen dollars, ten dollars, five dollars—which the son was to tell his mother the priest had given to his father. In short, the father was a compulsive liar.

Having been thrown out of the house by his wife, and having lost his job and pension, at the age of fifty-eight this man finally decided to quit drinking. He has now gone almost three years without a drink, has a little job, and lives in a small room all alone. His wife speaks with him occasionally though she doesn't see him. The son wishes his father well but doesn't want to see him. "I understand, but I won't forgive," the son said.

Scripture Selection

Genesis 2:18-24

[18]Then the Lord God said, "It is not good for the man to live alone. I will make a suitable companion to help him." [19]So he took some soil from the ground and formed all the animals and all the birds. Then

he brought them to the man to see what he would name them; and that is how they all got their names. ²⁰So the man named all the birds and all the animals; but not one of them was a suitable companion to help him.

²¹Then the Lord God made the man fall into a deep sleep, and while he was sleeping, he took out one of the man's ribs and closed up the flesh. ²²He formed a woman out of the rib and brought her to him. ²³Then the man said,

"At last, here is one of my own kind—
Bone taken from my bone, and flesh from my flesh.
'Woman' is her name because she was taken out of man."

²⁴That is why a man leaves his father and mother and is united with his wife, and they become one.

Mark 3:31-35

³¹Then Jesus' mother and brothers arrived. They stood outside the house and sent in a message, asking for him. ³²A crowd was sitting around Jesus, and they said to him, "Look, your mother and your brothers and sisters are outside, and they want you."

³³Jesus answered, "Who is my mother? Who are my brothers?" ³⁴He looked at the people sitting around him and said, "Look! Here are my mother and my brothers! Whoever does what God wants him to do is my brother, my sister, my mother."

Comments on Scripture Selection

God's creation of woman reinforced the overall goodness of His creation (see Gen. 1:31). Man was incomplete and needed "a suitable companion to help him" (Gen. 2:18). This expression in verse 18 means "a helper corresponding to him" or "a helper alongside of him." God intended the relationship between husband and wife to meet the basic human need of love and companionship.

Verses 19-20 show that none of the animals or birds was a suitable companion to man. The woman was a suitable helper because she was built from a portion of man's side and shared the same physical nature (see vv. 21-24). This text focuses upon the similarity of man and woman and on their mutual need of each other.

Genesis 2:18-24 recognizes that human life is inherently social and needs human relationships for satisfactory development. Marriage is a fundamental response to the need for companionship. The first song in the Bible was sung by man in celebration over God's gift of a wife (see v. 23). "One" in verse 24 refers to the one-flesh sexual union which bonds the personhood of marriage partners, but it carries with it the larger meaning of the whole human being rather than merely the sensual or physical aspect of human nature.

Mark 3:31 may tie back to 3:21. Perhaps His family had come to rescue Jesus from the consequences of His popularity and success or from the hands of His enemies (see Mark 3:20-30).

Jesus was not putting down the family in Mark 3:31-35, either His own family or family life in general. The four Gospels present evidence that Jesus was deeply devoted to His family (see Luke 2:39-52; John 19:25-27). He knew that the most precious and closest human relationships were inside the family. But Jesus calls us to even dearer relationships inside His forever family who do "what God wants" (v. 35). All those who follow the purposes and intentions of God are linked with Jesus as His family. His mother and brothers and sisters are those "who hear the word of God and obey it" (Luke 8:21).

Questions to Think About

• Two very different patterns of family life are presented in the two opening stories. Which of these stories is more like my childhood?

• Is there some wrong or hurt for which I haven't yet been able to forgive both or one of my parents?

• While marriage is a fundamental response to the human need for companionship, do I see anything in Genesis 2:18-24 which would rule out the larger family concept of parents, brothers and sisters, spouse, children, and in-laws as the basic social unit within which personality development takes place?

• According to the comments above on the Scripture selection, the first song in the Bible was sung in celebration of what gift from God?

• Mark 3:31-35 refers to the mother, brothers, and sisters of Jesus. What else may I learn about the family life of Jesus from Matthew 13:53-58 and from Luke 2:39-52?

• Based on the comments above on Mark 3:33-35, and on my own understanding of that passage of Scripture, what is the other family —of even dearer relationships—to which Jesus referred?

• In the light of Mark 3:31-35, how can it be said that Jesus Christ has done more to enhance and improve family life than any other individual?

Conclusion

The Bible is high on the need for family life. God Himself began the institution of the family according to Genesis 2:18-24. Also, according to Mark 3:35, "Whoever does what God wants" is a member of the "family of God" (see Eph. 2:19).

14

The Need for Friends

Can it be true that a dog is a person's best friend?

On the front lawn of the old Johnson County courthouse in Warrensburg, Missouri, stands a life-size statue of a hound dog named Old Drum. This statue stands as a tribute to faithful dogs everywhere. When it was dedicated some thirty years ago, thousands of people jammed the streets for the ceremony. Each year thousands of others journey to this small college town to view the bronze statue.

Old Drum was killed October 28, 1869. He had been the constant companion of a farmer named Charlie Burden. Burden's brother-in-law and neighbor, Leonidas Hornsby, ordered one of his hired hands to shoot Old Drum because he claimed the dog was bothering his sheep.

Four bitterly fought court trials were fought over the killing of Old Drum. Burden was determined to vindicate his dog. George Graham Vest, the attorney for Burden, made a spontaneous final appeal to the jury. "The best friend a man has in this world may turn against him and become his enemy. His son or daughter that he has reared with loving care may prove ungrateful," said Vest. "The one absolutely unselfish friend that a man can have in this selfish world," continued the eloquent attorney, "the one that never deserts him, and the one that never proves ungrateful or treacherous, is his dog."

The whole thing came to an end on September 23, 1870, in a crowded courtroom. Within minutes of Vest's speech on a dog being a man's best friend, the jury gave a unanimous verdict in favor of Burden. He was awarded fifty dollars for the loss of Old Drum.

The two attorneys and each of their law partners, who represented Burden and Hornsby, went on to achieve fame and high political offices. But only Old Drum was enshrined.

Whether it is really true that a dog is a person's best friend, one thing all of us know for certain is that we need a friend. None of us is strong enough to make it alone in life. Even Robinson Crusoe had his animals and his man Friday.

Pultizer Prize-winning author Frances Fitzgerald, in her book *Cities on a Hill,* surveyed four contemporary American cultures. One of those cultures was Sun City Center, a town near Orlando, Florida, composed entirely of senior citizens. Fitzgerald found a general preference in Sun City Center for cremation over burial. One citizen tried to explain the preference for cremation like this: "I don't have anyone. And my husband doesn't either, so there's no one to keep up the graves." If for no other reason, some persons need a friend just to keep up their graves when they are dead and gone.

Scripture Selection

1 Samuel 18:1-4

¹Saul and David finished their conversation. After that, Saul's son Jonathan was deeply attracted to David and came to love him as much as he loved himself. ²Saul kept David with him from that day on and did not let him go back home. ³Jonathan swore eternal friendship with David because of his deep affection for him. ⁴He took off the robe he was wearing and gave it to David, together with his armor and also his sword, bow, and belt.

John 5:1-9

¹After this, Jesus went to Jerusalem for a religious festival. ²Near the Sheep Gate in Jerusalem there is a pool with five porches; in Hebrew it is called Bethzatha. ³A large crowd of sick people were lying on the porches—the blind, the lame, and the paralyzed. ⁵A man was there who had been sick for thirty-eight years. ⁶Jesus saw him lying there, and he knew that the man had been sick for such a long time; so he asked him, "Do you want to get well?"

⁷The sick man answered, "Sir, I don't have anyone here to put me in the pool when the water is stirred up; while I am trying to get in, somebody else gets there first."

⁸Jesus said to him, "Get up, pick up your mat, and walk." ⁹Immediately the man got well; he picked up his mat and started walking.

Comments on Scripture Selection

First Samuel 18:1-4 depict the beginning of a classic friendship between David and Jonathan. Read 1 Samuel 20:1-42; 2 Samuel 1:17-27; and 9:1-13, in order to understand the depth of their friendship. The exchange of clothing and armor in verse 4 was a common way to seal a new friendship.

Strong relationships outside of one's own family are approved and encouraged in Scripture. Jonathan did not let his father's jealousy of David destroy the bonds and obligations of friendship. Wise parents will encourage and free their children to develop strong friendships outside the family. Families that have outside friendships are usually happier and healthier in their own relationships.

You may wish to read all of John 5:1-18 in order to get the full story on the healing at the pool of Bethzatha. A comparison between this healing and that of a paralyzed man, whom four determined friends took to Jesus, may also give you a better feel for this story (see Mark 2:1-12; Matt. 9:1-8; and Luke 5:17-26).

This invalid believed in the healing power of the waters. We are not told how long he had waited beside the pool, only that he had been helpless for thirty-eight years (v. 5). That's a very long time to wait on a cure, which was reflected in the question of Jesus: "Do you want to get well?" (v. 6).

I am struck by the first part of the sick man's answer, "Sir, I don't have anyone" (v. 7). No longer could he say that. Jesus had sought him out from among the "large crowd of sick people" (v. 3). A friend had come to help him—not to help him into the water but to heal him physically and spiritually (v. 14).

"Immediately the man got well" (v. 9), wrote the fourth evangelist. And he got well at the word of Jesus, by obeying His command (vv. 8-9).

The last half of verse 9 and on through verse 18 make much of the fact that this healing occurred on the Sabbath day. Can we not see in this miraculous cure that Jesus Christ is indeed "Lord of the Sabbath" (Matt. 12:8), Lord over physical paralysis, and Lord over all?

Questions to Think About

• Can an animal ever be as suitable a friend as another human being?

• How did David show his friendship with Jonathan even after Jonathan's death (see 2 Sam. 1:17-27; and 9:1-13)?

• With how many friends do I have the same quality of relationship as that which existed between Jonathan and David?

• The senior citizen of Sun City Center, quoted by Fitzgerald above, said something quite like the sick man at the pool of Bethzatha. What was it?

- The enemies of Jesus accused Him of being "a friend of tax collectors and other outcasts" (Matt. 11:19). Based on John 5:1-9 and other similar Scriptures, was this charge true?
- Proverbs 17:17 reads, "Friends always show their love. What are brothers for if not to share trouble?" Am I *that* kind of friend?
- The motto of Vidalia onions is, "They only make you cry when they're gone." Would that be a suitable motto for friends?

Conclusion

The ancient hymn "St. Patrick's Breastplate" ends with an acclamation praising Christ as one who comes to meet us "in mouth of friend and stranger." All three major festivals of the church—Christmas, Easter, and Pentecost—have to do with the advent of a Divine Stranger. "In each case," wrote John Koenig, "the newcomer offers blessings that cannot at first, be comprehended. The child in the manger, the traveler on the road to Emmaus, and the mighty wind of the Spirit all met us as mysterious visitors challenging our belief systems even as they welcome us to new worlds."

15

The Need for a Sense of Place

Without a sense of place it is almost impossible to know who we are. That's one reason I like to go back to Florence County, South Carolina, and visit the places where I lived in my childhood.

When Pope John Paul II returned to his native land of Poland, following his election to the papacy, he knelt down and kissed the ground. Every true patriot naturally loves the land of his or her birth. A refugee from Vietnam, one of the boat people now living in California, told interviewers: "You're not talking to me, I'm dead. My soul died in Vietnam. You're talking to the shell of my body. I'm dead."

The human being can stand just so much change. Already we are suffering from what Alvin Toffler called *future shock,* because the future is zooming in upon us with such speed. This future shock is caused in part by what Jacques Ellul called technique and what others simply called technology. On top of all that, the average American moves thirteen times in one lifetime. A sense of place adds stability in a world dizzy with change.

Most persons emphatically do not think of prison as a place where they would like to live. A thirty-year-old man was released from prison in North Carolina in 1982. He had served three years of a two-hundred-year sentence. The judge released him because of new evidence which showed that the man was not guilty. One comment by the released prisoner was to the effect that prison is a life of order without purpose and dreams without plans. That's the way most persons feel about life behind bars.

On the other hand, "Uncle John" Davis was sentenced to life imprisonment in 1922 for stealing a watch and five dollars. He was still in prison on his 105th birthday. State officials told Davis years ago that he could leave the maximum security Central Correctional Institution in Columbia, South Carolina. However, he has chosen to stay. His security rating has allowed him to come and go at will. "There's (sic) some men on the streets of Columbia who's (sic) free as running water," said Davis, "and they can't do half of what I can." Say whatever you will about the warped system of justice which sentenced a man to life imprisonment for stealing a watch and five dollars but don't overlook the powerful sense of place expressed in "Uncle John" Davis's decision to remain behind bars.

A Spanish proverb says, "Habits are at first cobwebs, then cables." Could it be that there is also something seductive about a sense of place?

Scripture Selection

Psalms 137:1-9

¹By the rivers of Babylon we sat down;/there we wept when we remembered Zion./²On the willows near by/we hung up our harps./ ³Those who captured us told us to sing;/they told us to entertain them:/"Sing us a song about Zion."

⁴How can we sing a song to the Lord/in a foreign land?/⁵May I never be able to play the harp again/if I forget you, Jerusalem!/⁶May I never be able to sing again/if I do not remember you,/if I do not think of you as my greatest joy!/

⁷Remember, Lord, what the Edomites did/the day Jerusalem was captured./Remember how they kept saying,/"Tear it down to the ground!"/

⁸Babylon, you will be destroyed./Happy is the man who pays you back/for what you have done to us—/⁹who takes your babies/and smashes them against a rock.

John 1:45-46

⁴⁵Philip found Nathanael and told him, "We have found the one whom Moses wrote about in the book of the Law and whom the prophets also wrote about. He is Jesus son of Joseph, from Nazareth."

⁴⁶"Can anything good come from Nazareth?" Nathanael asked. "Come and see," answered Philip.

Comments on Scripture Selection

A sense of place is very strong in the Bible. The origins of the Christian religion are connected with particular places such as Bethlehem, Nazareth, and Jerusalem.

Psalm 137 is about the destruction of Jerusalem and the Babylonian Exile of the Jewish people. The psalmist gave voice to the feelings that surged in the souls of many Jewish patriots during the Exile.

Verses 5-9 invoked four curses, "May I never be able to play the harp again/if I forget you, Jerusalem!" (v. 5). The psalmist did not stop with the invocation of *one* curse upon himself. A *second* curse was pronounced: "May I never be able to sing again/if I do not remember you,/if I do not think of you as my greatest joy!" (v. 6).

A *third* curse (v. 7) was then invoked against the Edomites who rejoiced when Jerusalem was destroyed in 587 BC. The Edomites were, of course, descendants of Esau, the brother of Jacob. One might have thought that these blood brothers to Judah would have at least wept over the destruction of Jerusalem. Instead, the Edomites said: "Tear it down to the ground!" Such treachery was unpardonable and the Jews' hatred of it undying. Apparently the prophecy of Obadiah, the shortest book in the Old Testament, was uttered in response to the gloating of the Edomites over the destruction of Jerusalem.

Still a *fourth* curse was invoked in verses 8 and 9. This time the curse was on Babylon, the destroyer of Jerusalem. This fourth curse took a ghastly turn in that a blessing was invoked upon those who in implementing it wiped out the breed forever: "Happy is the man . . ./who takes your babies/and smashes them against a rock."

Psalm 137 is unique. It is indeed a cursing, or imprecatory, psalm— probably the only true example of its kind in the Hebrew songbook. It is more than a lamentation over an experience of distress or persecution or bitterness of soul; this particular weeping (see v. 1) resorted to a curse as a means of defense or revenge.

Verse 4 is the key verse of the whole psalm: "How can we sing a song to the Lord/in a foreign land?" Verses 1-3 give the setting for that question while verses 5-9 lend strength and substance to it.

The first thing these Jews of the Dispersion did was sit down and weep. "By the rivers of Babylon we sat down;/there we wept when we remembered Zion" (v. 1). "The rivers of Babylon" were the great rivers of the Tigris and the Euphrates. "The willows" of verse 2 would have been the poplars.

Before persons can sing the Lord's song in any strange land, they have to deal with their grief and anger. One appropriate way to deal with grief and anger is to sit down and weep as did these Jewish patriots.

Anger and grief are not the same thing, but they are often partners as they are in Psalm 137. Note that the anger seen in Psalm 137 is sublimated in the imprecatory poetry of the psalmist. Nevertheless, it is expressed in the four curses of verses 5-9, and in the first person. Look at how the psalmist shifted from the first person plural "we" of verses 1-4 to the first person singular "I" in verses 5 and 6.

John 1:45-46 was one link in a chain of witnesses to Jesus Christ in this chapter. Here Philip witnessed to Nathanael. Philip testified that he and others—presumably Andrew, Peter, and another unnamed disciple of Jesus—had found Jesus of Nazareth about whom Moses and the Hebrew prophets wrote.

Nathanael's response was, "Nazareth! Can anything good come from there?" (v. 46, NIV). Apparently, Nazareth of Galilee was as despised by some Jews in the first century AD as Jerusalem was loved. Philip invited Nathanael to come and see for himself if anything good could come out of the hometown of Jesus.

Verses 47-51 indicate that Nathanael became a convinced follower of Jesus. "Teacher, . . . you are the Son of God! You are the King of Israel!" (v. 49) was his confession of faith. Pilate's sign over the cross of Jesus read: "Jesus of Nazareth, the King of the Jews" (John 19:19).

Questions to Think About

- What does my sense of place have to do with knowing who I am?
- Why is Jerusalem so important to Jews, Christians, and Muslims?
- The earth's population exceeded five billion on July 7, 1986, according to the Population Institution in Washington, D.C. Does my sense of place have anything to do with the number of persons on planet Earth?
- One way the dispersed Jews of Psalm 137 dealt with their grief and anger toward their captors was to sit down and weep. Is that an appropriate response for me to make in dealing with my anger and grief in my own "Babylonian captivity?"
- The psalmist sublimated his grief and anger in a special kind of poetry and by invoking four curses. Is that, or some other creative way, an appropriate way for me to deal with my anger and grief?
- Psalm 137 begins so nobly and ends so brutally. How do I account for that?

- Can I think of a time when I was seduced by a false and un-healthy sense of place?
- Why did Nathanael change his evaluation of Nazareth?

Conclusion

Where would you rather live: in Kennesaw, Georgia, which has a law requiring every ablebodied resident to own a loaded gun; or in Morton Grove, Illinois, which bans handguns? I think my choice would be to live in Acworth, Georgia, which requires all households to own fishing poles.

There is a black spiritual which says, "Sometimes I feel like a motherless child . . . a long way from home." Have you ever felt like that? If so, did it make you want to say, "This world is not my home; I'm just passing through?" Or, did that feeling make you want to hear God say what He said to Moses from the burning bush: "Take off your sandals, because you are standing on holy ground" (Ex. 3:5)?

PART IV
ESTEEM NEEDS

16

The Need for Human Dignity

There is a tale that goes something like this. An old man lived with his son and daughter-in-law. He was hard of hearing, blind, and had difficulty eating without spilling food. Sometimes he would drop a dish and break it. The son and his wife thought such conduct was disgusting. They made him eat in a corner behind the stove. He had to eat out of a wooden bowl that wouldn't break.

One day this old man's little grandson was working with wood. The boy's father asked him what he was going to do with the wood. "I'm making a trough for you and mother to eat out of when I'm grown up," replied the son.

Many of the elderly persons in our society need nothing so much as dignity. Look at "Miss Mary," a seventy-nine-year-old lady in Boston who lives in a small apartment, all alone. She has no one to care for her because she never married. Eight years ago she left Haiti to come to America with her nephew. Last year the nephew died. Now "Miss Mary" is alone, struggling to survive. Her greatest worry, beyond food for the day, is affording the cost of burial.

One senior adult seemed to catch something of the universal longing for a certain quality of life in the words of this anonymous poem:

> When I was young,
> I dreamed of the many goals I must reach;
> The great deeds I must accomplish;
> And the important things I must possess;
> Now I know there is only one great thing:

To live,
And see the great light which fills the world.

Rosa Parks is certainly no seventy-five-year-old female black Rambo. She's not even a grandmotherly version of Martin Luther King, Jr. But almost half her life ago in Montgomery, Alabama, this quiet lady asserted her dignity and claimed her right to sit wherever she pleased on a public bus.

This now-stooped old lady certainly did not set out to spark a civil-rights revolution. She was simply tired from a long day's work as a clerk at a department store, and she was tired in her soul at being abused all her life by racism—tired of being denied her human dignity. In fact, she was just too tired to obey the vile and demeaning command of a white bus driver, "Niggers move back!"

Parks's act was unintended, barely conscious. She herself observed: "I just wanted to go home to my family, to do what I needed to do for them. I didn't get on the bus intending to get arrested." But get arrested she did, and for no other reasons than her skin was black and the degrading law required that blacks sit in the back of the bus.

Could it be that a part of "the great light which fills the world," to which the anonymous poet referred, is human dignity? "The power of social change and the glue of social cohesion reside in the common people," wrote Don Covil Skinner, "not in the influence or rhetoric of charismatic leaders or cosmetic heroines." Rosa Parks was a ray of sunlight casting light and energy upon a dark place in America.

Scripture Selection

Genesis 1:26-31

[26]Then God said, "And now we will make human beings; they will be like us and resemble us. They will have power over the fish, the birds, and all animals, domestic and wild, large and small." [27]So God created human beings, making them to be like himself. He created them male and female, [28]blessed them, and said, "Have many children, so that your descendants will live all over the earth and bring

it under their control. I am putting you in charge of the fish, the birds, and all the wild animals. [29]I have provided all kinds of grain and all kinds of fruit for you to eat; [30]but for all the wild animals and for all the birds I have provided grass and leafy plants for food"—and it was done. [31]God looked at everything he had made, and he was very pleased. Evening passed and morning came—that was the sixth day.

Romans 5:6-11

[6]For when we were still helpless, Christ died for the wicked at the time that God chose. [7]It is difficult thing for someone to die for a righteous person. It may even be that someone might dare to die for a good person. [8]But God has shown us how much he loves us—it was while we were still sinners that Christ died for us! [9]By his death we are now put right with God; how much more, then, will we be saved by him from God's anger! [10]We were God's enemies, but he made us his friends through the death of his Son. Now that we are God's friends, how much more will we be saved by Christ's life! [11]But that is not all; we rejoice because of what God has done through our Lord Jesus Christ, who has now made us God's friends.

Comments on Scripture Selection

If Genesis 1:26-31 is compared with the preceding verses of chapter 1, one may see that God's creation of the world and everything in it moves from the general to the specific, and from the lower to the higher. Human beings are the crowning act of God's work. Unique characteristics of God are bestowed upon them alone.

"They will be like us and resemble us" (v. 26) and "making them to be like himself" (v. 27), that's the way *The Good News Bible* describes the uniqueness of human beings. Both the King James Version and the Revised Standard Version use the words *image* and *likeness* to translate the Hebrew word *tselem*. The plural "we" and "us" of verse 26 may be nothing more than the plural of majesty. It was customary for rulers to refer to themselves in the plural as well as in the singular.

While some degree of physical likeness is implied, the divine image included a delegated stewardship over the natural world (see vv. 26 and 28). Human beings were given power over all fish, birds, and animals and put in charge of them. Just as God took control of the formless and desolate earth and moved it to order and form, so humans are to take an unfinished and untamed creation and direct it and subdue it as God's managers.

Both male and female reflect and reveal their Creator's characteristics. Therefore, the image of God may also be revealed in the male-female relationship of love and commitment (see vv. 27-28). God's blessing, mentioned in verse 28, was actually a part of His salvation. God reveals Himself through the loving commitment of one human being for another.

The basis for defining human personhood is the image of God. Persons are created with the capacity for relationship with God and with one another. This makes family life and community life possible.

Romans 5:6-11 takes us much farther along the way in the biblical story of God's blessings and goodness upon the human race. The great fall in the garden (see Gen. 3) and the great rebellion at the Tower of Babel (see Gen. 11) have long since taken place. Humans have become "sinners" (v. 8), "wicked" (v. 6), "God's enemies" (v. 10), subject to "God's anger" (v. 9). They are "helpless" (v. 6) to save themselves from their bondage to sin and evil or from the consequences of their disobedience and rebellion against God.

So, what happened? That's what Romans 5 is all about. "God has shown us how much he loves us" (v. 8) by sending Jesus Christ, His son, to put us "right with God" (v. 9), to make us "his friends through the death of his Son" (v. 10), to save us right now and in the future from God's anger (v. 9).

The path to human dignity has been fought in the realm of law dealing with human rights, but ultimately it begins and ends in the study of God. Human dignity arises out of being created in the image of God and the fact that Christ died for all. That is the combined message of Genesis 1:26-31 and Romans 5:6-11.

Questions to Think About

• Is human dignity something persons earn, or is it a free gift from God?

• According to Genesis 1:27-28 and to the opening tale about the old man, from whom do children tend to learn their first lessons about human dignity?

• Do I believe that all persons are of infinite worth and value whatever their age, sex, race, occupation, nationality, religion, or other identifying characteristics?

• How does the Scripture selection from Genesis 1 and Romans 5 support or encourage the action of Rosa Parks?

• Do I personally know anyone like "Miss Mary" of Boston?

• Why is the power and control which God gave human beings in Genesis 1 often exercised so brutally?

• Through what historical event did God prove the length, depth, breadth, and height of His love for human beings, according to Romans 5:6-11?

Conclusion

If God esteems us so highly that He created us in His own mental and moral likeness, and loves us so much that "while we were still sinners . . . Christ died for us" (Rom. 5:8), why don't we think more highly of ourselves, of others, and of Him?

17

The Need for Respect

Actor Rodney Dangerfield has made famous and funny the saying, "I don't get no respect."

When Norman Vincent Peale's little daughter, Margaret, was about five years old, he was awakened one morning by the sound of her voice from the nursery next to his room. It must have been about six o'clock. Margaret was carrying on a great conversation with herself, interspersed with bubbling laughter.

Peale went into the nursery and interrupted her monologue by saying: "Margaret, this is a strange time for you to be talking so noisily to yourself. You are disturbing everybody who is trying to sleep in this house. Furthermore," her father continued, "it seems to me rather foolish for you to lie there talking to yourself and laughing at your own remarks."

"Oh, Daddy," said Margaret in that tone which only children can use to put parents in their place, "Oh Daddy, you don't understand. I have an awful good time with myself."

Margaret's kind of healthly self-respect is sorely needed. Fortunately, self-esteem can be learned and enhanced, no matter how low it may be.

"I've finally done something in my life!" said the thirty-five-year-old mother of four as her children clung to her long black gown. What had Elyse Sanchez done? She had graduated *summa cum laude* with a straight-A average from Lehman College in the Bronx. But that wasn't all. Seventeen years earlier she had dropped out of college, and four years after her husband left her she had gone on welfare. Even so, there was still something else that Elyse Sanchez had done to be so pleased with herself at her graduation. She had tried on her new self-respect and found that it fit just right.

Another aspect of respect is respect for others. C. Oscar Johnson, a pastor whom I much admired, told many years ago how he learned a painful lesson about respect for others. He was presiding in a service at Third Baptist Church, Saint Louis, Missouri, when a woman tiptoed in, craned her neck to locate a seat, stepped across several people and shimmied a bit to settle into a barely adequate space on the pew. Johnson impulsively came out with, "If you leave home on time, you get to church on time!"

While standing at the door shaking hands and absorbing compliments, he saw that woman approach him saying something like this: "Oh, Dr. Johnson, I am so sorry I was late today. For the past six months I have been nursing my invalid mother, but I decided this morning I couldn't stand not being at church any longer, so I got a neighbor to stay with Mama long enough for me to be here!"

"I wanted the floor to open and swallow me!" wailed the pastor.

Scripture Selection

Psalms 8:3-8

[3]When I look at the sky, which you have made,/at moon and the stars, which you have set in their places—/[4]What is man, that you think of him;/mere man that you care for him?/[5]Yet you made him inferior only to yourself;/you crowned him with glory and honor./[6]You appointed him ruler over everything you made;/you placed him over all creation:/[7]sheep and cattle, and the wild animals too;/[8]the birds and the fish/and the creatures in the seas.

Romans 12:3-10

[3]Because of God's gracious gift to me I say to every one of you: Do not think of yourself more highly than you should. Instead, be modest in your thinking, and judge yourself according to the amount of faith that God has given you. [4]We have many parts in the one body,

and all these parts have different functions. [5]In the same way, though we are many, we are one body in union with Christ, and we are all joined to each other as different parts of one body. [6]So we are to use our different gifts in accordance with the grace that God has given us. If our gift is to speak God's message, we should do it according to the faith that we have; [7]if it is to serve, we should serve; if it is to teach, we should teach; [8]if it is to encourage others, we should do so. Whoever shares with others should do it generously; whoever has authority should work hard; whoever shows kindness to others should do it cheerfully.

[9]Love must be completely sincere. Hate what is evil, hold on to what is good. [10]Love one another warmly as Christian brothers, and be eager to show respect for one another.

Comments on Scripture Selection

Psalm 8 is a song of praise to God for His greatness as seen in His creation of nature and humankind. Particularly does this hymn reflect the place of human beings in the scheme of creation. It is a poetical echo of Genesis 1 and a hymn of contrasts. Verses 3-4 contrast God's greatness and man's littleness; whereas verses 5-8 contrast mankind's relation to God and to their own natural world.

The psalmist in verses 3-4 was contemplating the heavens at night. Their vastness, order, and beauty deepened his sense of human insignificance before God. Reflecting on the immeasurable greatness of God moved the psalmist to exclaim, "What is man, that you think of him;/mere man, that you care for him?" (v. 4). Both "man" and "mere man" in verse 4 refer to humankind in the collective sense. God not only thinks of human beings, He cares for them in the sense of paying them a tender and gracious visitation in order to make up for whatever may be missing or lacking in them (see v. 4).

Verse 5 reveals that as insignificant as humans are they are no accident in the creation. Like the sky, the moon, and the stars of verse 3, they were made by God for a high purpose. That purpose was to be a king and God's deputy "over all creation" (v. 6).

"Inferior only to yourself" in verse 5 may mean inferior only to

beings such as angels, or inferior only to God Himself. "Crowned
. . . with glory and honor" were words commonly used with reference
to kings. Man's lordship over the creation (see vv. 6-8) pointed to his
royal status.

Romans 12:3-10 are some verses lifted out of Paul's practical instructions to Christians in Rome. Chapters 12—15 of Romans seek
to answer the question: What should be the daily life of those who
have been saved by faith in Jesus Christ?

Verses 3 and 10 have particular relevance to respect. Verse 3 implied that there were followers of Jesus in Rome who thought too
highly of themselves. Perhaps they thought themselves superior to
other Christians because of the more "showy" gifts which they had.
Verses 4-8 may be read that way.

Paul's point in verse 3 was that Christians should think of themselves "according to the amount of faith God has given you." Faith,
as used here, meant power given by God to do a certain thing (see
1 Cor. 13:2). So Paul seemed to be saying that persons' opinions of
themselves should be in proportion to God's gifts and not to their
natural abilities. If all would follow that rule, there would be no room
for boastful pride because none of us has anything which he or she
did not receive (see 1 Cor. 4:7). Those who are genuinely humble
before God are unlikely to be arrogant before their fellow creatures.

The unity of the church as the body of Christ requires that Christians not be arrogant but humble and loving toward each other.
Therefore, verses 4-10 give the reason for Paul's instruction in verse
3. God's gifts are not given for self-congratulation but for building
up the body. Authentic love will "be eager to show respect for one
another" (v. 10).

Questions to Think About

- Is it really funny when I feel that "I don't get no respect"?
- Do I, like five-year-old Margaret, "have an awful good time with
myself"? If not, why don't I?
- Can I think of several times in my life when, like Elyse Sanchez,
I have put on self-respect and found that it fit just right?

• A newspaper headline read, "Korea Hopes to Win Respect at Olypmics." Can persons, like nations, win the respect of others?

• Has there been a particularly painful time in my life when, like C. Oscar Johnson, I failed to show respect for someone else and wanted the floor to open and swallow me?

• How many reasons can I find in Psalm 8:3-8 for respecting myself and others?

• While Romans 12:3-10 instructs Christians not to think more highly of themselves than they should, and to show respect for one another, can I find anything at all in that passage which approves an inferiority complex in a Christian or in anybody else?

Conclusion

"Son, always remember who you are," said Henry Grady's mother as he was leaving home for the city one morning. Long after he became a famous newspaperman, Grady recalled that his mother had taught him so well that he could never forget those words.

God has told us who we are in Psalm 8 and Romans 12. If we remember as well as did Grady, we shall respect ourselves and others.

18

The Need for Status

"Everyone will be a celebrity for fifteen minutes," said the late artist Andy Warhol.

Celebrity status may now be sought in such unusual ways as collecting credit cards. Walter Cavanagh has gotten himself certified by the Guinness Book of World Records as the world's champion credit-card collector. Cavanagh, according to the latest count, owned

1,099 credit cards. He never leaves home without a bunch of them. Each month he applies for 100 cards and gets few refusals. He can't get enough of the handy little plastics. Call him "Mr. Fantastic Plastic," because that's what he calls himself.

Sergeant Alvin C. York, who died in 1964, won his status as the most celebrated American hero of World War I. This sharpshooter from the Tennessee backwoods single-handedly silenced a German battalion of thirty-five machine guns. He killed twenty-five enemy soldiers, and with the help of his squad, captured 132.

French Marshal Ferdinand Foch told York, "What you did was the greatest thing accomplished by any private soldier of all the armies of Europe." If you go to Chatel-Chehery, France, you can find a simple monument to Sgt. York's incredible feat on October 8, 1918, in the Argonne Forest.

Two other things combined to make York's deeds so daring. "For someone to knock out a machine-gun nest with a pistol and a five-shot rifle was really a symbol of the individual standing up to the machine age," said Russell Hippe, chairman of the Tennessee Historical Commission. Also, York's pacifist beliefs almost kept him out of the war.

By all accounts York was a modest man. He shunned offers of commercial endorsements that would have made him rich. Instead, he settled down to a life of blacksmithing, hog farming, and running a grist mill.

But journey with me in your mind to a jail in Chicago. It's winter time and very cold. Watch two kind policemen charge a homeless man with the crime of begging just so they can get him a warm place to rest overnight in a city jail. The jailor is a god in that place. He talks so tough he leaves bite marks on his curses. All the prisoners are under his power, and they had better not forget it.

Listen to the six or so cops at the lockup desk. They use their ounce of power to wield their way on the prisoners. See the low-life guards as they miss no opportunity to let the wretched prisoners know that there is at least one underclass lower than guards.

Then, go on to a cell block made for two but housing four, with two thick boards called beds—no sheets, pillows, or blankets. Which two of those four cell mates will be lucky enough to get the two thick boards called "beds"? You guessed right; it depends upon their status.

Scripture Selection

Genesis 37:3-11

[3]Jacob loved Joseph more than all his other sons, because he had been born to him when he was old. He made a long robe with full sleeves for him. [4]When his brothers saw that their father loved Joseph more than he loved them, they hated their brother so much that they would not speak to him in a friendly manner.

[5]One time Joseph had a dream, and when he told his brothers about it, they hated him even more. [6]He said, "Listen to the dream I had. [7]We were all in the field tying up the sheaves of wheat, when my sheaf got up and stood up straight. Yours formed a circle around mine and bowed down to it."

[8]"Do you think you are going to be a king and rule over us?" his brothers asked. So they hated him even more because of his dreams and because of what he said about them.

[9]Then Joseph had another dream and told his brothers, "I had another dream, in which I saw the sun, the moon, and eleven stars bowing down to me."

[10]He also told the dream to his father, and his father scolded him: "What kind of dream is that? Do you think that your mother, your brothers, and I are going to come and bow down to you?" [11]Joseph's brothers were jealous of him, but his father kept thinking about the whole matter.

Philippians 2:3-11

[3]Don't do anything from selfish ambition or from a cheap desire to boast, but be humble toward one another, always considering others better than yourselves. [4]And look out for one another's interests, not just for your own. [5]The attitude you should have is the one

Christ Jesus had:/⁶He always had the nature of God,/but he did not think that by/force he should try to/become equal with God./⁷Instead of this, of his own free/will he gave up all he had,/and took the nature of a servant./He became like man/and appeared in human likeness./⁸He was humble and walked/the path of obedience all the way to death—/his death on the cross./⁹For this reason God raised him/to the highest place above/and gave him the name that/is greater than any other name./¹⁰And so, in honor of the name of Jesus/all beings in heaven, on earth, and in the world below/will fall on their knees,/¹¹and all will openly proclaim that Jesus is Lord,/to the glory of God the Father.

Comments on Scripture Selection

Read Genesis 37:3-11 for what the passage may teach about the struggle for status in Jacob's family. Jacob showed the same kind of favoritism to Joseph which his mother, Rebecca, had shown to him (see Gen. 27:5-17). This storyteller was an artist of the first rank.

Often Jacob felt inferior, even when his fortunes were superior. He had always wanted to have the status in his family which belonged to Esau, his older twin brother (see Gen. 27—28). By patience and craftiness, and with his mother's help, Jacob had gained the standing in the family which should have by legal rights gone to Esau. But Jacob was never certain he had succeeded. Was the "long robe with full sleeves" (v. 3) for Joseph a symbol for the status he himself had wanted?

Naturally, Joseph's brothers were upset that he was their father's pet (see v. 4). Nor did Joseph's two dreams (see vv. 5-11) do anything but cause them to hate him more.

Philippians 2:3-11 were written against a background of petty jealousies over status among Christians in the church at Philippi (see Phil. 4:2-3). It was taken for granted in the Greek culture of Paul's time that persons ought to assert themselves, and only fools and cowards would yield of their own accord to any rival.

Instead, Paul taught that the followers of Christ should "be humble toward one another" (v. 3). The word translated "humble" literally means "lowly minded." Paul was saying that when it comes to favors, or claims to outward distinctions, Christians should consider others better than themselves. He was not saying they should falsely depreciate their own merits and abilities.

The main thrust of this passage is that when it comes to the question of status among Christians, they are to have the same attitude which Christ Jesus had (v. 5). Verses 6-8 reveal that Christ was so lowly minded that although "He always had the nature of God" (v. 6), He "took the nature of a servant" (v. 7), and "was humble . . . all the way to death—his death on the cross" (v. 8).

Verses 8-11 show that as a result of Christ's humiliation, He was given a higher place than He had before. Through His humble service, Jesus pleased the Father, who made Him ruler of the universe.

Questions to Think About

• Do I want some kind of celebrity status? If so, what kind of celebrity do I want to be?

• How well do I think Sgt. York handled his celebrity status?

• What was the "pecking" order at the jail on South State Street in Chicago?

• Tacitus once remarked, "The lust for power, for dominating others, influences the heart more than any other passion." What evidence can I point to in Genesis 37 and Philippians 2, or in the contemporary examples cited above, which support this remark by Tacitus?

• Does the Bible condone parents showing favoritism toward one child over their other children?

• In light of Genesis 50:15-21, did the young man Joseph of Genesis 37 really want his brothers to bow down before him? What particular interpretation do I give to Genesis 50:20 with regards to the two dreams of Joseph in Genesis 37:5-11?

• How well do I think Paul's words in 2 Corinthians 8:9 express this main thought in Philippians 2:3-11?

Conclusion

Status seeking, and the never-ending struggle for standing among others, appears to be an inseparable part of the story of the human race. Whether gotten by hook or crook, status will be gotten; and it will be used to bless or to curse. Both Joseph and Jesus used their status to bless the human race.

19

The Need for Recognition

Not yet in kindergarten, Ashton, age three, has a clothes closet stocked with nothing but the best. He has forty-two-dollar flannel shirts, eighty-dollar imported Tartine et Chocolat wool sweaters, designer polo shirts, and a one-hundred-fifty-dollar winter coat for those days when San Francisco weather turns nasty.

Label consciousness now begins in preschool. It gets worse as kids get older. One fourth grader, who had been shunned for months by her classmates, was taken aside by a classmate who whispered, "You'll make more friends if you wear Esprit clothes."

"Kids are wearing miniversions of what their parents do," said the owner of a clothing store in Massachusetts. The manager of a fashionable clothing store more bluntly said, "Their children are status symbols. When their children wear designer clothes, it's like their driving a Mercedes—they want to turn heads."

For those who can't afford that kind of money in order to gain recognition from others, what about a much cheaper religious version? It's a $1.98 ballpoint pen, topped with the tiny carved figure of a rabbit, which bears the inscription: "Jesus thinks you're somebunny special!"

Now contrast the above kinds of recognition with that given to Winnie Pearce who died in 1987. Many years ago, in Chicago, Winnie enrolled in a religious drama course under the direction of the renowned dramatist Fred Eastman. The class presented a dramatic presentation, and Winnie auditioned for the role of a Southern "mountain woman." Winnie got the part, reached back into her heritage, and portrayed the role out of her own history.

On opening night, she and the cast had stage fright. But when Eastman slipped backstage and told them the playwright was in the audience, they were paralyzed with fear. When the curtain went down, the author went backstage and spoke gracious words of commendation to each member of the cast. But when he came to Winnie, the "mountain woman," he took both her hands in his and said, "My dear, tonight you have put into flesh and blood the woman I dreamed on paper."

But for still another kind of recognition, call to your mind Emily in Thornton Wilder's *Our Town*. Emily, who died as a young wife and mother, asked to come back to Grover's Corners to relive her twelfth birthday. The others, sitting in the graveyard scene, tried to discourage her, but she came back for a day.

"Oh, Mama," she cried when she saw the familiar figure going about her day carelessly and casually, "Oh, Mama, just look at me one minute as though you really saw me."

Scripture Selection

Jeremiah 1:4-10

⁴The Lord said to me, ⁵"I chose you before I gave you life, and before you were born I selected you to be a prophet to the nations."

⁶I answered, "Sovereign Lord, I don't know how to speak; I am too young."

⁷But the Lord said to me, "Do not say that you are too young, but go to the people I send you to, and tell them everything I command

you to say. [8]Do not be afraid of them, for I will be with you to protect you. I, the Lord, have spoken!"

[9]Then the Lord reached out, touched my lips, and said to me, "Listen, I am giving you the words you must speak. [10]Today, I give you authority over nations and kingdoms to uproot and to pull down, to destroy and to overthrow, to build and to plant."

John 1:47-51

[47]When Jesus saw Nathanael coming to him, he said about him, "Here is a real Israelite; there is nothing false in him!"

[48]Nathanael asked him, "How do you know me?"

Jesus answered, "I saw you when you were under the fig tree before Philip called you."

[49]"Teacher," answered Nathanael, "you are the Son of God! You are the King of Israel!"

[50]Jesus said, "Do you believe just because I told you I saw you when you were under the fig tree? You will see much greater things than this!" [51]And he said to them, "I am telling you the truth: you will see heaven open and God's angels going up and coming down on the Son of Man."

Comments on Scripture Selection

Jeremiah recounted his call to be a prophet of the Lord in 1:4-10. Aside from the other features of his call, look in particular at God's recognition of Jeremiah. God "chose" him before he was born (see Isa. 49:1,5; Gal. 1:15). What an awesome knowledge that must have been!

Jeremiah in verse 5 may have been trying to convey the inescapability of his being chosen. Some persons don't want to be known that well by God. As Sören Kierkegaard said, "It is most comfortable to stride unknown through the world, without being known to His Majesty the King."

The youth protested his immaturity in verse 6. The word "young" in verses 6 and 7 may mean a "child," as translated by the King James Version, or a "youth" as translated by the Revised Standard Version.

Most likely the Hebrew word refers to a young person and indicates immaturity. But we cannot from verses 6 and 7 derive the exact age of Jeremiah when he was called.

Another indication of God's recognition of Jeremiah was that the Lord "touched" his lips (v. 9). This symbolic action was important because the Hebrew prophet was believed to be himself a mouthpiece for God (see Jer. 15:19). God's touch made his lips clean and his mouth pure (see Isa. 6:7).

Jeremiah's call to be a prophet to the nations and to Israel came out of a meeting with the living God. Nothing less than the absolute conviction that God had sent him to the people would have sustained him in his formidable task (see vv. 7-8).

John 1:47-51 may be an earlier example of what is written in 2:25. Jesus knew human nature very well. That was hinted at when He changed Simon's name to Cephas or Peter, meaning "a rock" (John. 1:42).

Jesus praised Nathanael, who had belittled His origin. He recognized Nathanael, who was from nearby Cana in Galilee (see John. 21:2), as the model pious Jew in the Old Testament (see Mic. 4:4; Zech. 3:10).

Jesus read Nathanael like some persons read a book. He knew that here was a man in whom there were no hidden motives, no deceit. Nathanael was transparent to Jesus.

The style of life which Nathanael most passionately wanted was described by Jesus in that high compliment of verse 47. Needless to say, Nathanael was surprised: "How do you know me?" (v. 48). The second half of verse 48 gave the answer. Jesus had seen Nathanael much as He had earlier seen Simon (v. 42).

Verses 49-51 show the response which Nathanael made to Jesus' recognition of him. "Teacher" in verse 49 was a title of respect which a disciple would use. "You are the Son of God!" was quite different than "son of Joseph" in verse 45. While Nathanael might not have understood the full implications of the title, he knew that Jesus enjoyed a special relationship with God (see Ps. 2:7).

According to verse 50, Nathanael became a believer in Jesus (see

John 20:31) and began to follow Him as one of His disciples. Jesus promised him that he would see "greater things."

Verse 51 may recall Jacob's dream at Bethel in Genesis 28:10-22. Jacob called Bethel "the house of God" and "the gate that opens into heaven" (Gen. 28:17). Here Jesus claimed to be "the house of God," the place of meeting with the Father, and "the gate that opens into heaven." In other words, Jesus claimed that He Himself was the ladder between heaven and earth. This means that He claimed to be the personal channel of revelation between God and persons. That was at least a part of the "much greater things" Nathanael would see.

Questions to Think About

- What kind of recognition do I *want* right now?
- What kind of recognition do I *need* most?
- Can I recall a time when I received a similar kind of recognition to that which Winnie Pearce received for playing the part of the "mountain woman"?
- Do I identify strongly with the feelings expressed by Emily in Thornton Wilder's *Our Town?* If so, why? and if not, why not?
- Am I frightened or comforted at the thought that God may know me as well as He knew Jeremiah?
- Do I believe that Jesus sees and compliments me like He did Nathanael in John 1?
- Does Jesus want me to give Him a similar kind of recognition to that which He received from Nathanael?

Conclusion

Martin of Tours illustrates the spirit which should mark our recognition of others. Martin was a Roman soldier and a Christian believer. On a cold winter day as he entered a city, a beggar asked him for alms.

Martin had none but he was moved by the sight of the beggar, blue and shivering from the intense cold. He removed his coat, worn and tattered though it was, cut it into two equal pieces and gave one to the beggar.

That night he had a dream. In it he saw the angels in heaven with Jesus in their midst. He was wearing half of a Roman soldier's cloak.

"Why are You wearing that tattered old coat?" an angel asked. "Who gave it to You?"

And Jesus responded softly, "My servant Martin gave it to Me."

20

The Need to Feel Useful

Lois Dixon, teacher, boss, and friend to Renee Prim, said of her: "It's almost as though she doesn't want to admit there isn't anything she can't do."

Prim had been paralyzed eleven years earlier by a fall from a playground ride. The accident happened when she was twenty-one. Married just six months, Prim was a carefree student with long, blond hair who loved to dance. She and her husband were celebrating moving into a new apartment. They got on the children's merry-go-round and started spinning. Prim lost her grip and fell backwards.

Later, she passed out, and a blood clot was found at the top of her spine. They shaved off her beautiful hair, so surgeons could remove the clot. A foot-long scar was left on her bald head. She was paralyzed. Neither her kidneys, bowels, legs, or arms worked. Through therapy she regained use of her left arm and partial use of her right. But she could never walk again.

Her marriage fell apart, and she moved back in with her parents. For three months, Prim said, "The only thing I wanted to do was cry and sit and watch TV."

When the crisis had passed and she was all cried out, what did Prim do? She went back to school. Prim earned three associate degrees from Central Piedmont Community College in Charlotte, North Carolina. She also finished a bachelor's degree at the University of North Carolina in Charlotte.

Today Prim works full time as a lab instructor and supervises three persons. She types thirty-five words per minute with her left hand, sews, bakes, gardens, and repairs broken computers.

In addition to all that, Prim hung the wallpaper in her kitchen, laid the carpet in her spare bedroom, and repaired the cracked concrete in her front walk. She owns her own home. It has no ramps, grab bars, or any other special devices for the handicapped. "If you have a ramp, you're going to get lazy," said Prim. The words *I can't* are not in this lady's vocabulary.

Add to the story of Renee Prim the testimony of Olympic gold medal winner Greg Louganis. Louganis has proven that there are very few things he can't do as a swimmer. Yet he told the world in 1988 why a few years earlier he had stopped smoking and drinking. After he had won his first gold medals, he went out to the parking lot one day to take a smoke. A twelve-year-old kid was standing there smoking. Louganis asked him what he was doing. The lad answered, "I know you smoke, and I want to be just like you when I grow up." Stunned, Louganis realized that whether he wanted to be or not, he was a role model to youngsters. He decided then and there to quit smoking and drinking.

Scripture Selection

Ruth 2:10-13

¹⁰Ruth bowed down with her face touching the ground, and said to Boaz, "Why should you be so concerned about me? Why should you be so kind to a foreigner?"

¹¹Boaz answered, "I have heard about everything that you have done for your mother-in-law since your husband died. I know how you left your father and mother and your own country and how you came to live among a people you had never known before. ¹²May the Lord reward you for what you have done. May you have a full

reward from the Lord God of Israel, to whom you have come for protection!"

¹³Ruth answered, "You are very kind to me, sir. You have made me feel better by speaking gently to me, even though I am not the equal of one of your servants."

Luke 10:38-42

³⁸As Jesus and his disciples went on their way, he came to a village where a woman named Martha welcomed him in her home. ³⁹She had a sister named Mary, who sat down at the feet of the Lord and listened to his teaching. ⁴⁰Martha was upset over all the work she had to do, so she came and said, "Lord, don't you care that my sister has left me to do all the work by myself? Tell her to come and help me!"

⁴¹The Lord answered her, "Martha, Martha! You are worried and troubled over so many things, ⁴²but just one thing is needed. Mary has chosen the right thing, and it will not be taken away from her."

Comments on Scripture Selection

You may wish to read Ruth 1:1 through 2:9 in order to get the setting for Ruth 2:10-13. Ruth was a Moabite who had married an Israelite. That's the reason she called herself "a foreigner" in verse 10. Ruth, her sister Orpah, and their mother-in-law Naomi were all widowed (Ruth 1:3-5).

Naomi, "left all alone, without husband or sons" (v. 5) in a foreign land, decided to return to Judah. Ruth came back with her, embraced Naomi's people and her God, and Ruth vowed she would never leave Naomi (Ruth 1:16-17). Still Naomi was very bitter (Ruth 1:20-21). Ruth's friendship and loyalty was the one bright spot in her mother-in-law's darkness and despair. They needed each other, and they both needed someone else to help them.

Boaz, a wealthy and influential relative of Naomi's husband, was the man whom God sent to help them (see Ruth 2:1-9). "It so happened" in verse 3 does not mean that it was only by chance Ruth gleaned in a field that belonged to Boaz.

Ruth's bowing down before Boaz in verse 10 was an expression of her humility. She was so amazed at Boaz's graciousness toward her that she bowed to the ground and asked him why. Boaz answered to the effect that it was because of what she had done for Naomi (v. 11). But he also emphasized Ruth's acceptance of the God of Israel (v. 12). Actually Boaz invoked a beautiful blessing on Ruth in verse 12, a blessing which he himself fulfilled when he became her husband (see 3:9).

Verse 13 was an expression of grateful surprise. Ruth was still an alien, even though she was under Boaz's protection.

The story of Martha and Mary in Luke 10:38-42 is found only in Luke's Gospel. However, the Gospel of John says these sisters and their brother Lazarus lived in the village of Bethany (John 11:1; 12:1-3). The Fourth Gospel also identifies the woman of Bethany who anointed Jesus shortly before His arrest (Mark 14:3) with the Mary of this story (John 12:3).

Martha and Mary were very different in the way they served Jesus. Martha, the mistress of the house, like Paul's married man and woman in 1 Corinthians 7:33-34 (RSV) was "anxious about worldly affairs"; whereas Mary, like Paul's unmarried woman, was "anxious about the affairs of the Lord."

If I have read verses 41-42 correctly, both Jesus and Paul, who had a higher view of women than that held by their culture (see Gal. 3:28), wanted all women to give themselves "completely to the Lord's service without any reservation" (1 Cor. 7:35). Jesus did not follow His culture, which limited the role of women. He gently rebuked Martha for her excessive attention to housework and commended Mary for her attention to spiritual growth.

This story teaches that as important as food is to physical life, spiritual food is even more important. Why be "worried and troubled" (v. 41) over so many dishes of good food, when a few or really one dish would be sufficient (v. 42)? Isn't "the right thing" (v. 42)— the very best dish of all—to hear "the words that give eternal life" (John 6:68) from Jesus Himself?

Questions to Think About

- Like Renee Prim, can I feel useful in spite of my handicaps?
- When Greg Louganis realized he was a role model to youngsters, did he become more or less useful to them?
- What have I done lately to make myself feel more useful to others?
- Renee Prim said: "At times I feel more sorry for people who can walk. Because they're griping and groaning, when they should be smiling." How do I react to that statement, coming from one who said her greatest accomplishment since being paralyzed was being able to tie her own shoes?
- In the story of Ruth, Naomi, and Boaz, who do I think felt more useful to whom?
- Am I surprised that Ruth, a Moabite woman, became the great-grandmother of David, Israel's greatest king, and ended up being included in the genealogy of Jesus (Matt. 1:5)?
- Am I more like Martha or Mary? Which of these sisters do I want to be more like?

Conclusion

Jesus was tempted by the devil to misuse His power and turn stones into bread. He answered with a quotation from Deuteronomy 8:3, "Man cannot live on bread alone, but needs every word that God speaks" (Matt. 4:4). Is it possible that in order to feel most useful to God and to others, we need to strike a better balance between Martha's concern for physical food and Mary's concern for spiritual food?

PART V
SELF-ACTUALIZATION NEEDS

21

The Need for Success

"A shortstop who can field an agitated horsefly!" That's the way veteran sportswriter Red Smith, who died in 1982, described Johnny Pesky, a Boston Red Sox player, in one of his early columns for the *New York Herald Tribune.* That kind of baseball playing and that kind of writing, point to *two* successful men.

Rudolph, the Red-Nosed Reindeer, as the whole world knows, is about a loser who became a winner. The assets of that shiny red nose were at first thought to be liabilities by almost everybody, including Santa Claus and Rudolph. But not nearly so many people know the real flesh-and-blood success story behind this ever-popular children's Christmas story.

The year was 1938. Robert L. May, age thirty-five, was heavily in debt. His wife was seriously ill, and he was trying to take care of their four-year-old daughter, Barbara. They lived in a dark little apartment on Chicago's north side.

Employed by Mongomery Ward in an advertising job he didn't like, May felt like a loser. He had been smart in school. In fact, he had graduated from high school at age fourteen and gone on to Dartmouth College. But he could not seem to find an outlet for his creativity in the real world. When Christmas of 1938 came and went, May was relieved because he had not felt much like celebrating.

Then came his big break. His boss wanted May to see if he could create a better booklet than those little Christmas giveaway coloring books his company had been buying from local peddlers. That's when May came up with his story whose main character would be a loser, like himself. But the character would in the end be successful. He would realize his own natural strengths and use them for a good cause.

May's boss turned him down flat when he first proposed the story. Later, he got some drawings and won the approval to proceed with the book. Through that winter and on into the summer, May wrote his story in longhand. Margaret was the one he tried it out on, to see if she understood the vocabulary.

His wife died in July, and May's boss offered to take him off the story. May insisted that he now needed to work on the project more than ever.

During the Christmas season of 1939, Mongomery Ward printed and handed out free 2.4 million copies of *Rudolph the Red-Nosed Reindeer.*

Rudolph's fame enabled May, who died in 1976, to move into a better house and to pay off his bills. "My dad always viewed Rudolph as a gift, something magical, and he refused to exploit it," said May's daughter, Barbara. "Rudolph's story was really my dad's own story," she continued. "They were both underdogs who learned to believe in themselves."

Scripture Selection

Genesis 24:12-21

[12]He prayed, "Lord, God of my master Abraham, give me success today and keep your promise to my master. [13]Here I am at the well where the young women of the city will be coming to get water. [14]I will say to one of them, 'Please, lower your jar and let me have a drink.' If she says, 'Drink, and I will also bring water for your camels,' may she be the one that you have chosen for your servant Isaac. If this happens, I will know that you have kept your promise to my master."

[15]Before he had finished praying, Rebecca arrived with a water jar on her shoulder. She was the daughter of Bethuel, who was the son of Abraham's brother Nahor and his wife Milcah. [16]She was a very beautiful young girl and still a virgin. She went down to the well,

filled her jar and came back. [17]The servant ran to meet her and said, "Please give me a drink of water from your jar."

[18]She said, "Drink, sir," and quickly lowered her jar from her shoulder and held it while he drank. [19]When he had finished, she said, "I will also bring water for your camels and let them have all they want." [20]She quickly emptied her jar into the animals' drinking trough and ran to the well to get more water, until she had watered all his camels. [21]The man kept watching her in silence, to see if the Lord had given him success.

Hebrews 12:1-2

[1]As for us, we have this large crowd of witnesses around us. So then, let us rid ourselves of everything that gets in the way, and of the sin which holds on to us so tightly, and let us run with determination the race that lies before us. [2]Let us keep our eyes fixed on Jesus, on whom our faith depends from beginning to end. He did not give up because of the cross! On the contrary, because of the joy that was waiting for him, he thought nothing of the disgrace of dying on the cross, and he is now seated at the right side of God's throne.

Comments on Scripture Selection

Read all of Genesis 24 in order to get the full story of how Rebecca became the wife of Isaac. Most early societies, including the society of Israel, gave dominant roles to men, whereas women were generally obscure. However, some women in the Old Testament were significant. Rebecca was one of them. She appears in this chapter as a person with rights (see vv. 55-61), although she was very respectful of her parents and all others as well.

Genesis 24:12-21 is a success story from ancient Israel. Twice, *The Good News Bible* uses the word *success* (vv. 12,21). Abraham's servant said, "The Lord has made my journey a success" (v. 56). The success referred to was that of finding a suitable wife for Abraham's son, Isaac.

Abraham's servant prayed for success in his mission (see vv. 12-15). He wanted God's will to be done in this important matter (see

v. 14). Yet, the servant also employed his own intelligence and common sense (see vv. 15-21). His choice of Rebecca was ultimately based on her character as well as on God's specific leadership. See Rebecca's natural charm and winsomeness in verse 16, her quick and kind friendliness in verse 18, her happy heartedness and generosity in going above and beyond the call of duty in verses 19-20.

Hebrews 12:1-2 depict the Christian life as "the race that lies before us" (v. 1). This race is more like a marathon relay race in which the people of God are all runners who keep passing the torch of faith from one another to the next generation.

The "large crowd of witnesses" (v. 1) were those referred to in Hebrews 11. They were the faithful runners who had already successfully finished their part of God's relay race. Their faithfulness in running the race of life was cited as an incentive to the success of those who followed in their path.

Athletes do not go out to run dressed in their heavy clothes and overshoes. On the contrary, they strip themselves of all excess baggage and lay aside everything that would hold them back. Likewise, the writer of Hebrews urged his readers, "Let us rid ourselves of everything that gets in the way, and of the sin which holds on to us so tightly" (v. 1).

Verse 2 lifts up the crucified and exalted Jesus as the supreme example of the kind of "determination" (v. 1) which persons need in order to successfully finish God's marathon. Jesus, "on whom our faith depends from beginning to end. . . . did not give up because of the cross!" (v. 2). Nor should we who face much lesser obstacles ever quit the race, the author strongly implies (see also vv. 3-4).

Questions to Think About

• Why do the words *A shortstop who can field an agitated horsefly* point to *two* successful men?

• Why do I think the story of *Rudolph, the Red-Nosed Reindeer* has been so phenomenally successful?

• What role did each of the following items play in the success of

Robert L. May: creativity, determination, the illness and death of his wife, taking care of his four-year-old daughter, Barbara?

• With which character do I identify most in the story behind the story of Rudolph, and why?

• Do I believe that God is concerned about human success in such earthly things as choosing a marriage partner?

• In the success story of how Rebecca was chosen to be Issac's wife, and based on the comments above on Genesis 24:12-21, what are two lessons which may be learned about success from this story?

• To whom does Hebrews 12:2 point as the supreme example of success in the race of life?

Conclusion

Granted that success is needed by all, how can we measure it? Dean Smith, University of North Carolina basketball coach at Chapel Hill, said the way to measure success is to "do what you can with what you have . . . where you are." Coach Smith thinks society ought to shrug off the fantasy that success is gauged by material wealth. He believes failure is relative to one's perspective, to time, and to one's use of failure.

Smith ought to know what he's talking about. After a losing basketball season in 1961, angry students hanged him in effigy. Yet, when he gave a lecture on success in 1985, his teams had won twenty or more games each year for the past nineteen seasons. That made him the fourth-most-successful coach in college basketball history.

22

The Need to Realize One's Highest Potential

Composer Darius Milhaud has written over four hundred works. Someone asked him, "If you had to go to a desert island, which of your compositions would you take with you?" Milhaud replied, "I'd take some blank paper. My favorite composition is always the one I will write tomorrow."

That's the kind of attitude persons have who realize their highest potential. It was the attitude expressed by Jascha Heifetz, the Russian-born virtuoso whose name was synonymous with violinistic perfection for more than half a century. "There is no such thing as perfection," said Heifetz, "there are only standards. And after you have set a standard, you learn that it was not high enough. You want to surpass it."

Heifetz made his public debut at age seven. He practiced on his violin six hours or more every day while enrolled at Saint Petersburg Conservatory in Russia during his youth. By 1919, he was the highest-paid violinist in history, receiving $2,250 for one concert. Although, he never claimed perfection in his work, Heifetz did set the standards of excellence by which all later violinists would be measured.

Persons who realize their highest potential frequently push themselves to the limit. Pete Maravich, shortly before his death at age forty, said his dad's dream and his own dream was "to take the game of basketball and push it to the limit." That meant that Maravich spent six to ten hours a day with a basketball in his hands. At age twelve, on Saturday afternoons when other kids were out swimming, playing, and having a good time, Pete was in the gym playing basketball all day long.

Perhaps nobody ever worked at basketball harder than this kid. He dribbled through his house blindfolded, would take an aisle seat and dribble during a movie, would hang out the car window and dribble as his father drove the family car at varying speeds, dribbled while riding his bicycle, and even dribbled through mud puddles during a violent thunderstorm.

A friend once bet him he couldn't keep a ball spinning constantly for an hour. Pete spun the skin off his fingertips, knuckles, and thumbs. He also collected the five-dollar bet.

Knowing all of that about Pistol Pete Maravich, should anyone be surprised that he became one of the most prolific scorers in the history of basketball? He averaged 44.5 points during one college season, became a two-time NBA All-Star, and the NBA scoring champ in 1977.

Scripture Selection

Psalms 1:1-6

1Happy are those/who reject the advice of evil men,/who do not follow the example of sinners/or join those who have no use for God./2Instead, they find joy in obeying/the law of the Lord,/and they study it day and night./3They are like trees that grow/beside a stream,/that bears fruit at the right time,/and whose leaves do not dry up./They succeed in everything they do.

4But evil men are not like this at all;/they are like straw that the wind blows away./5Sinners will be condemned by God/and kept apart from God's own people./6The righteous are guided and/protected by the Lord,/but the evil are on the way to their doom.

Philippians 3:12-16

12I do not claim that I have already succeeded or have already become perfect. I keep striving to win the prize for which Christ Jesus has already won me to himself. 13Of course, my brothers, I really do not think that I have already won it; the one thing I do, however, is to forget what is behind me and do my best to reach what is ahead. [14]So I run straight toward the goal in order to win the prize, which is God's call through Christ Jesus to the life above.

[15]All of us who are spiritually mature should have this same attitude. But if some of you have a different attitude, God will make this clear to you. [16]However that may be, let us go forward according to the same rules we have followed until now.

Comments on Scripture Selection

Psalm 1 is life's "two-ways" psalm—the ways of life and death. It introduces us to the evergreen soul. Jeremiah 17:5-8 says essentially the same thing as this psalm, but in a different way. Happy and blessed persons are those who put their trust in God; whereas, on the other hand, evil and condemned persons are those who put their trust "in man,/in the strength of mortal man" (Jer. 17:5).

"Happy" in verse 1 is translated as "Blessed" by both the King James Version and the Revised Standard Version. The Hebrew psalmist used the plural form to magnify his thought and to make it almost the equivalent of an exclamation. It may be translated, "Oh, the happinesses of." Therefore, in the eyes of this songwriter, persons who reached their highest happiness were those described in verses 1-3.

Those who "succeed in everything they do" (v. 3) were those described negatively in verse 1 and positively in verses 2-3. They "find joy in obeying the Law of the Lord,/and they study it day and night" (v. 2).

"Law" literally meant *teaching, instruction,* or *direction.* The idea of a command comes from that meaning. The Hebrews used the word to refer to the first five books of the Old Testament or the law of Moses. In time, "law" came to refer to all the books of the Old Testament, and even later it came to mean God's will as revealed in nature, history, conscience, experience, and worship.

Persons who realized their highest potential were those who continually thought on the Word, will, and ways of God. They were those who thought God's thoughts after Him. They could count on God's guidance and protection throughout their existence (v. 6).

The word "perfect" is a major clue to understanding Philippians 3:12-16. You will find it in verses 12 and 15, although *The Good News Bible* translates it as "spiritually mature" in verse 15.

"Perfect" comes from the Greek root *teleios* and has a variety of meanings. In most of the places where it is used in the New Testament, the word does not mean philosophical and abstract perfection. Usually it signifies a functional perfection, or an adequacy for some specific purpose. As used in verses 12 and 15, the word means full grown or spiritually mature.

Paul was saying in verse 12 that he did not claim to be a fully grown or complete Christian. What he did claim was that he was the athlete of Christ (see vv. 12-14). As a foot runner for Christ, he single-mindedly kept his eyes on the prize with his whole being striving to reach the goal "which is God's call through Jesus Christ to the life above" (v. 14).

Paul refused to live in the past or to bask in prior accomplishments (see vv. 1-11). He would never glory in his previous achievements or rest upon his laurels.

Most likely, all of Philippians 3 should be understood as having been written against a background of antinomians in the church at Philippi. Antinomians were literally those against law. Apparently there were some Christians who denied that there was any law at all in the Christian life. They thought because they were already in Christ that it didn't matter what they did. These would have been the "many whose lives make them enemies of Christ's death on the cross" (v. 18).

Paul contended that all Christians "who are spiritually mature" (v. 15) should have the same attitude which he expressed in verses 12-14. To the end of the day of the Christian life, insisted Paul, Christians should see themselves as Christ's athletes and recognize the further discipline and effort required in order to reach their highest potential.

Questions to Think About

• How does my attitude toward realizing my highest potential differ from that of composer Darius Milhaud?

• Does what violinist Jascha Heifetz said about perfection square with Paul's teaching on perfection in Philippians 3:12-16?

• Pete Maravich pushed himself to the limit in the game of basketball. For what have I pushed myself to the limit?

• Who was the psalmist talking about when he said, "They succeed in everything they do" (Ps. 1:3)?

• How is Jeremiah 17:5-8 different from Psalm 1?

• Am I like the evergreen soul described in Psalm 1?

• How does the phrase "athlete of Christ" fit me?

Conclusion

Archibald Rutledge was in the back country when he became confused about his roads and asked a man how to get to Charleston. The man replied in his vernacular speech: "Cap'n, if you really wants to go to Cha'son, you mustn't start from here."

Contrary to those directions, if we are really serious about setting out on a journey to realize our highest potential, the only place we can start is right here where we are.

23

The Need for Meaning

She was a death rocker, age twenty-one, who wore black clothes and had dyed black hair. Her face was painted ghostly white. A shadowy figure called "Mr. Death" was tatooed on her right shoulder. Tragedy and comedy masks were tatooed on her left arm. She lived in a bedroom painted black and decorated with skulls and other symbols of the underworld.

Her name was Laura K., better known to her friends as "Lore Nell," queen of the death rockers. Like most of her friends, Laura had rejected—and been rejected by—mainstream society. She saw little hope for the future. Like most death rockers, she had turned to music to express her feelings of alienation and despair. Her music was more discordant than punk rock, the lyrics more depressing, and the album covers had scenes of death and violence.

On July 31, 1988, Laura jumped from an eleven-story building and killed herself. A suicide note was found in her apartment which explained that she didn't want to go on living. She saw no reason; life was futile.

One of Laura's friends said, "She was tired of being broke and in the position of having to scrounge around, not being able to go anywhere or do anything for lack of money." Another friend expressed the wish, "If she's in heaven, I hope she's got some good drugs and beautiful lovers and killer music."

Shift with me now from that heavy story of personal tragedy, and what it may symbolize, to another lighter and much more hopeful story about the search for meaning.

Edmond Rostand, a French playwright and poet, wrote a play titled *Chanticleer*. The play is about a magnificient rooster named Chanticleer. Rostand's rooster would hop off his roost every morning about dawn, station himself in the barnyard, and crow loudly as the sun came up. Each day Chanticleer congratulated himself on his melodious crowing with its powerful effect upon the sun.

One morning the proud old bird overslept. When Chanticleer opened his bleary eyes, lo and behold, the sun was already up!

Right then this lovely feathered creature, who imagined himself to be king of the barnyard, made a profound discovery. His crowing had no effect whatsoever on the sun's coming up! Even if he didn't crow, the sun would still rise.

So, smart and resourceful bird that he was, he determined that if his crowing didn't make the sun rise, he would nevertheless crow because it was up! Next morning, following his usual pattern, Chanticleer stationed himself at his place in the barnyard and joyfully crowed because the sun was up. Even in his disappointment, he found something about which to crow.

Scripture Selection

Deuteronomy 30:19-20

[19]"I am now giving you the choice between life and death, between God's blessing and God's curse, and I call heaven and earth to witness the choice you make. Choose life. [20]Love the Lord your God, obey him and be faithful to him, and then you and your descendants will live long in the land that he promised to give your ancestors, Abraham, Isaac, and Jacob."

Ephesians 1:8-14

In all his wisdom and insight [9]God did what he had purposed, and made known to us the secret plan he had already decided to complete by means of Christ. [10]This plan, which God will complete when the time is right, is to bring all creation together, everything in heaven and on earth, with Christ as head.

[11]All things are done according to God's plan and decision; and God chose us to be his own people in union with Christ because of his purpose, based on what he had decided from the very beginning. [12]Let us, then, who were the first to hope in Christ, praise God's glory!

[13]And you also became God's people when you heard the true message, the Good News that brought you salvation. You believed in Christ, and God put his stamp of ownership on you by giving you the Holy Spirit he had promised. [14]The Spirit is the guarantee that we shall receive what God has promised his people, and this assures us that God will give complete freedom to those who are his. Let us praise his glory!

Comments on Scripture Selection

Read Deuteronomy 29:1 through 30:20 to get the whole sermon which Moses preached to the people of Israel about renewing their covenant with God. According to 30:11-20, God's covenant gave His people the choice between faith/life or rebellion/death. Joshua later made a similar call to Israel (see Josh. 24:1-28).

Verses 19-20 were the concluding words spoken by Moses before the people of Israel publicly assumed their vows to keep God's covenant. Moses gave the people a clear and free "choice between life and death, between God's blessing and God's curse" (v. 19). Earlier, in verse 15, the choice was said to be "between good and evil." Those who chose to obey God's covenant were choosing good which was the path to God's blessing of life. Those who chose not to obey God's covenant were choosing evil which was the path to God's curse of death. Because of the covenant aspect of Israel's faith, it was impossible to enter into this covenant relationship with God, with one another, and remain neutral toward idols or sentimentally tolerant toward evil.

The choice set before Israel was so solemn that the whole hosts of "heaven and earth" (v. 19) were called to witness the true nature of the alternatives. Genuine religion calls persons to "Sell all you have . . . then come and follow me" (Luke 18:22).

Ephesians 1:9-10 is the key to understanding verses 8-14. The writer of this book was not afraid of cosmic visions. He here insisted that Christ is the answer to all the questions humans can ask.

Verses 8-10 teach that God has an eternal plan "to bring all creation together, everything in heaven and on earth" (v. 10) "by means of Christ" (v. 9). God has made known to Christians His "secret plan" (v. 9) to sum up all things "with Christ as head" (v. 10). Furthermore, "God's plan and decision" (v. 11) has been, is now being, and will be completed in time and history (see Gal. 4:4).

However, the phrase "when the time is right" (v. 10) would be more accurately translated "the times." The New Testament idea of time carries with it the idea of a succession of seasons or world periods. Each season of time has been marked by decisive events which determine its character, and each contributes to the succeeding age. Therefore, from the point of view of the New Testament writers, the Christian era is represented as the last in a series of ages, inaugurated by the incarnation, crucifixion, resurrection, and ascension of Christ—but consummated in the second coming of Christ to Earth.

Verses 11 and 12 point to the "union with Christ" (v. 11) of Jewish believers, such as the apostle Paul, as a stage in the fulfillment of God's divine purpose for all creation. Verses 13-14 point to the salvation of Gentile believers in Christ as another stage in the completion of God's long-range plan for the ages.

Questions to Think About

• Philosopher Friedrich Nietzsche wrote: "If we have our own why of life, we shall get along with almost any how." Based on what was said above about Laura K., do I think she had her "own why of life"?

• Is my personal "why of life" strong enough to enable me to "get along with almost any how"?

• Do I think Laura K.'s problem was "being broke" and "lack of money," as one of her friends suggested?

• What kind of message about meaning do I believe death rockers like Laura K. and her friends are trying to convey to mainstream society?

• If Rostand's *Chanticleer* may be thought of as a humorous story that's really about persons instead of roosters, and if I am Chanticleer, do I "crow" to make the sun come up or because it does comes up? Do I celebrate life because of my own illusions or because of what God does?

• Do I face a similar choice to that of Israel in Deuteronomy 30? What does my choice have to do with the meaning of life?

• Does God's plan for the ages, sketched in Ephesians 1:8-14, make sense to me?

Conclusion

"Meaning makes a great many things endurable," said famed psychoanalyst Carl G. Jung, "perhaps everything." Some persons, like Laura K., never find enough meaning to make everything in their lives endurable. Others, like Rostand's cocky rooster, discover something to really crow about. They find the "life in all its fullness" (John 10:10) which Jesus said He came to give.

24

The Need for Beauty

The need for beauty may be one of the things that makes humans different from all other animals. Keats spoke truly when he said, "A thing of beauty is a joy forever:/Its loveliness increases; it can never/ Pass into nothingness." If the writer of Proverbs could have passed judgment on this saying of the poet, would he not have concluded that "An idea well-expressed is like a design of gold, set in silver" (Prov. 25:11)?

Katherine Cook, a social worker, sought to discover all those things her spirit could not live without. What she noticed first of all was color. "I love colors—in sunsets, flowers, balloons, stained-glass with the sun streaming through, clothing, window curtains, and impressionist paintings," said Cook. Then, she concluded, "Colors—vivid, brilliant splashes of colors—are essential . . . to my . . . health."

I was not surprised to read that Cook felt she could not live without the ministry of colors to her spirit. Long ago, South Carolina's poet laureate, Archibald Rutledge, wrote in his book *Life's Extras* that the color scheme of the universe was one of life's extras. God might have chosen to make the world just one color like olive gray. Instead, said Rutledge, He chose to create a place with all the colors of the rainbow in it.

In another book of his, *Home by the River,* Rutledge commented on how we carelessly think of some disaster as "an act of God." Yet, "all beauty is an act of God," he said. "And to plant a garden is to co-operate with the Creator. No one can ever bring loveliness into this world unless he is holding fast the hands of God."

If you want to see the kind of garden to which Rutledge was referring, take one of North Carolina's backroads in the area where Halifax, Bertie, Martin, and Edgecombe counties come close together. Turn at a country store, and behold what the hands of Mrs. Myrtle Simpson has wrought for more than fifty years. Instead of putting her flower garden right up beside her house, Mrs. Simpson has planted her flowers and blooming shrubs on the highway right of way, lining both sides of the two ditches in front of her house. Her flower garden is by the road where all passersby can enjoy it.

The workers who cut the grass along the side of the road love it. Litterbugs don't throw trash and bottles on it. One person who soaked up its beauty said, "It is like driving on the road to the Land of Oz." He even mused, "One person's ditch is another person's canvas."

Scripture Selection

Hosea 14:4-8

[4]The Lord says,/"I will bring my people back to me./I will love them with all my heart;/no longer am I angry with them./[5]I will be to the people of Israel/like rain in a dry land./They will blossom like flowers;/they will be firmly rooted/like the trees of Lebanon./[6]They will be alive with new growth,/and beautiful like olive trees./They will be fragrant/like the cedars of Lebanon./[7]Once again they will live under my protection./They will grow crops of grain/and be fruitful like a vineyard./They will be as famous as/the wine of Lebanon./[8]The people of Israel will have/nothing more to do with idols;/I

will answer their prayers/and take care of them./Like an evergreen tree I will shelter them;/I am the source of all their blessings."

Mark 14:3-9

[3]Jesus was in Bethany at the house of Simon, a man who had suffered from a dreaded skin disease. While Jesus was eating, a woman came in with an alabaster jar full of a very expensive perfume made of pure nard. She broke the jar and poured the perfume on Jesus' head. [4]Some of the people there became angry and said to one another, "What was the use of wasting the perfume? [5]It could have been sold for more than three hundred silver coins and the money given to the poor!" And they criticized her harshly.

[6]But Jesus said, "Leave her alone! Why are you bothering her? She has done a fine and beautiful thing for me. [7]You will always have poor people with you, and any time you want to, you can help them. But you will not always have me. [8]She did what she could; she poured perfume on my body to prepare it ahead of time for burial. [9]Now, I assure you that whenever the gospel is preached all over the world, what she has done will be told in memory of her."

Comments on Scripture Selection

Hosea 14:4-8 tells what God's response would be to Israel's return to Him (see Hos. 14:1-3). Israel had shown a harlot spirit toward God by going after idols (see v. 8). That spirit was like a disease of the soul which had separated the people of Israel from God. In verse 4, God in effect promised to heal His people of the sin of backsliding and faithlessness (see Ps. 103:3).

A noteworthy feature of verses 5-7 may be the positive use of figures drawn from nature to describe the newness of life and strength which God promised His people. They had turned away from faithfulness to the Lord through the seductions of nature worship (see Hos. 2:8-13). Now restored Israel would be like a beautiful garden, a lovely and fragrant forest, and a fruitful vineyard. The ugliness of their disease would be transformed into the beauty and blessings (v. 8) of the Lord.

"They will blossom like flowers" (v. 5) was a reference to the lilies of the field, or anemones, which grow profusely in Palestine. These lilies are wild, beautiful, and plentiful. The remainder of verse 5 and verse 6 call to mind Psalms 1:3. "Beautiful like olive trees" (v. 6) continues the figure of the firmly rooted trees which show their strength, beauty, and vigorous life. Fragrance, like beautiful-smelling perfume, is revealed in the scent of the cedars of Lebanon (v. 6) and in the wine (v. 7).

Israel's prosperity and wealth under God's protection (v. 7) sounds a bit like the garden which God planted in Eden (see Gen. 2:8-17). God Himself promised to shelter His people like an evergreen tree (v. 8).

The story of Mark 14:3-9 had as its setting the passion of Jesus. He was on His way to be crucified on a cross. "She poured perfume on my body to prepare it ahead of time for burial" (v. 8) refers to the forthcoming death and burial of Jesus.

Fortunately, we have three separate but parallel accounts of the "beautiful thing" this unnamed woman did for Jesus. The other two accounts may be found in Matthew 26:6-13 and in John 12:1-8. John's record identifies Judas Iscariot, the one who was going to betray Jesus (John 12:4-6), with Mark's "Some of the people" (Mark 14:4) who became angry at the woman. According to John 12:6, Judas Iscariot's motive for criticizing the woman was "not because he cared about the poor, but because he was a thief." That, at least, suggests that those who criticized the woman harshly were only uttering pious platitudes. They might have wanted to cover up their own lack of extravagant devotion to Jesus.

Jesus was the *Messiah,* a word which means the anointed one. This woman anointed Jesus with very costly perfume. One silver coin was what a laboring person earned for one day's work. Judas Iscariot and others condemned such lavish waste. But Jesus told them to leave her alone. In fact, He saw her action as a spontaneous act of love and highly commended her: "She has done a fine and beautiful thing for me" (v. 6).

This female disciple wasn't seeking fame; nevertheless, she received it (see v. 9). The story teaches that God's last word is not the clink of a coin, that self-forgetfulness and self-denial is a thing of beauty and a joy forever.

Questions to Think About

• Do I, like Katherine Cook, feel that I can't live without the ministry of color to my spirit?

• Can I agree with Archibald Rutledge that "all beauty is an act of God"?

• Am I doing whatever I can, like Myrtle Simpson, to provide a spot of beauty which others can enjoy?

• According to Hosea 14:4-8, is it possible for a whole people to become a thing of beauty and a joy forever?

• Based on what is written in Hosea 14:1-3, what did Israel have to do before God made her into a beautiful and fragrant garden?

• With whom do I identify most in Mark 14: the woman who anointed Jesus with very expensive perfume or the people who criticized her harshly?

• What "fine and beautiful thing" have I done, like the woman in Bethany, which might be worthy of God's "Well done" (Matt. 25:-21)?

Conclusion

"That which is striking and beautiful is not always good," said Ninon de l'Enclos, "but that which is good is always beautiful." The Wisdom Literature of the Hebrews expressed a similar thought in religious language: "Charm is deceptive and beauty disappears, but a woman who honors the Lord should be praised" (Prov. 31:30).

25

The Need for Hope

"I feel like a human being for the first time in my life," a sixty-five-year-old woman in Moscow told Robert McNeille. She was referring to the impact of new freedoms on her life in Russia under Mikhail Gorbachev. This was her first taste of human rights. But what hope is there for multiplied millions who are being denied their human rights the world over?

Think of Lech Walesa, leader of Poland's outlawed Solidarity labor movement. Since the founding of Solidarity in 1980, the eyes of the world keep turning to Walesa and his supporters. One young Solidarity leader in 1988 called Walesa's meetings with Communist Party officials in Poland, "Talk, talk, talk." Edward Jarek, another thirty-five-year-old member of the strike committee in the town of Jaruzelski bitterly summed up the Polish coal miners' disillusionment by saying: "I don't believe *any* communist regime can be reformed." Is there really any hope for the oppressed workers of Poland?

We don't have to go all the way to Poland, or behind the Iron Curtain, to see the need for hope. Go to the labor pools of almost Anycity, USA. Take Atlanta, a kind of capital city of the South. Two thousand men and some fifty women sit there in various downtown labor pools each morning. They are homeless.

Among them is Henry, who grew up in North Carolina and twenty years ago went to Atlanta in search of work and his shot at the American Dream. Henry is now a resident of nowhere, although he is a member of the human community which calls itself Atlanta. Henry has gone from job to job, as do most unskilled workers in our economy. He drinks alcohol to ease his pain and grasp once more at his dream. The place where he sleeps is under a bridge just off the interstate. His day begins at 5:00 AM, as he stumbles toward the local private enterprise labor pool.

Henry has to choose each day between whether to work or to go hungry. If he chooses to work and get his twenty-five-dollar pay check, he will have to pass up the opportunity for the two meals at the soup kitchens. This day his choice is to eat. But where will he relieve himself? There are no public toilets. He hopes no one will see him, but his bowels cry out. The church which gave him his breakfast has locked its doors. A momentary desire passed through the broken man's heart: "If only I had a few sheets of toilet paper, and maybe a piece of soap and a little water." He doesn't, so now he stinks.

Twice a week Henry sells his blood to a blood bank for eight dollars. As ironical as it may seem, according to Ed Loring, an advo-cate for the homeless in Atlanta, "the safest and most comfortable place for the homeless person in all of Atlanta is on the blood bank bed." But that lasts only four hours per week.

Scripture Selection

Psalms 42:1-11

[1]As a deer longs for a stream of cool water,/so I long for you, O God./[2]I thirst for you, the living God./When can I go and worship in your presence?/[3]Day and night I cry,/and tears are my only food;/ all the time my enemies ask me,/"Where is your God?"/

[4]My heart breaks when I/remember the past,/when I went with the crowds to the house of God/and led them as they walked along,/ a happy crowd, singing and shouting praise to God./[5]Why am I so sad?/Why am I so troubled?/I will put my hope in God,/and once again I will praise him,/my savior and my God./

[6-7]Here in exile my heart is breaking,/and so I turn my thoughts to him./He had sent waves of sorrow over my soul;/from Mount Hermon and Mount Mizar./[8]May the Lord show his constant love

during the day,/so that I may have a song at night,/a prayer to the God of my life./

⁹To God, my defender, I say,/"Why have you forgotten me?/Why must I go on suffering/from the cruelty of my enemies?"/¹⁰I am crushed by their insults,/as they keep on asking me,/"Where is your God?"/

¹¹Why am I so sad?/Why am I so troubled?/I will put my hope in God,/and once again I will praise him,/my savior and my God.

1 Peter 1:3-5

³Let us give thanks to the God and Father of our Lord Jesus Christ! Because of his great mercy he gave us new life by raising Jesus Christ from death. This fills us with a living hope, ⁴and so we look forward to possessing the rich blessings that God keeps for his people. He keeps them for you in heaven, where they cannot decay or spoil or fade away. ⁵They are for you, who through faith are kept safe by God's power for the salvation which is ready to be revealed at the end of time.

Comments on Scripture Selection

Psalms 42 and 43 have a shared theme, style, and refrain (see 42:5,11; 43:5). They are the prayer of a person in exile (vv. 6-7), and remind us of the words of Paul in 2 Corinthians 4:8, "often troubled, but not crushed; sometimes in doubt, but never in despair." Perhaps a feel for Psalm 42 might be gained by reading both Psalms 42 and 43 several times. Note how the refrain is thrice repeated in identical form. Also, compare 42:9 and 43:2 for their slight variations.

Psalm 42 is a personal lament which deals with personal distress and suffering. Verse 4, "I . . . led them as they walked along" suggests that the psalmist may have been a priest or a Levite. He appears to have been living in the region of the peaks of Hermon at Mount Mizar (vv. 6-7), cut off from God and country (see 42:1; and 43:3).

Mount Herman is literally "the Hermans." It is an area of rushing streams where melting snow creates madly tumbling cataracts that echo to each other, filing the ravines with the thunder of rushing water. That kind of geographical terrain and activity of nature fits well the phrase in *The Good News Bible:* "Sent waves of sorrow over my soul" (vv. 6-7). And it fits even better the Revised Standard Version's translation of verse 7, which reads: "Deep calls to deep at the thunder of thy cataracts;/all thy waves and thy billows have gone over me."

The enemies of the psalmist, who taunted him with the question, "Where is your God?" (vv. 3,10), were not clearly identified. Perhaps they were the Assyrians who invaded northern Israel or the Babylonians who invaded Judah. Whoever they were, they were cruel and insulting (vv. 9-10).

Like wild animals in a drought (see Joel 1:20), the psalmist thirsted after "the living God" (vv. 1-2). While that phrase—"the living God" —may mean the same as "the God of my life" (v. 8), it might have also been used to distinguish the God of the Hebrews from the gods of the nations who were so often wooden or stone idols without life. The God of the Hebrews was alive and active for His people.

This psalm reveals that in spite of the loneliness and suffering of this unknown Hebrew poet, he put his hope in God (vv. 5,11). And he generated hope in at least three ways: by talking to himself (vv. 5,11), by exercising his precious memory and turning his thoughts to God (vv. 4,6-7), and by speaking directly to God (v. 9).

First Peter was written to Christian exiles who lived as scattered refugees in the region known as Asia Minor (see 1:1). These followers of Christ were undergoing, or about to undergo, a fiery test of persecution and suffering for their faith (see 1:6 *ff.* and 4:12 *ff.*). But Peter did not open his book with a speech on suffering. Instead, he began it with a discussion of "a living hope" (v. 3). This discussion of living hope actually begins in verse 3 and continues on through verse 12.

What Peter called "living hope" comes from Jesus Christ the giver of "life-giving water" (John 4:7-15; 7:37-38). Indeed, Peter so closely tied God's gift of living hope to the "new life" (v. 3) in Christ and to God's "salvation" (v. 5) that it is securely anchored in God's "great mercy . . . by raising Jesus Christ from death" (v. 3).

Questions to Think About

• Based on what was said about the sixty-five-year-old woman in Moscow, the Polish workers connected with Solidarity, and the homeless in Atlanta, what connections (if any) do I see between human rights and hope, between human freedom and hope, and between human dignity and hope?

• The apostle Paul put faith, hope, and love together in 1 Corinthians 13:13. Poet Wallace Stevens said, "Nothing is itself taken alone. Things are because of interrelations and interconnections." In the light of both of these references, how do I see faith, hope, and love interrelating and interconnecting in the story of Henry?

• Is hope an ingredient needed only by down-and-outs like Henry, or is it also needed by up-and-outs in society?

• I read about a forty-two-year-old man in a state institution who had been there twenty years and was so lonely he wrote letters to himself. What evidences may I point to in Psalm 42 which indicate the psalmist was very lonely?

• According to Psalm 42 and the comments on that Scripture above, which of the three methods used by the psalmist to generate hope do I think is most satisfying?

• Do I see any connection between Peter's "living hope" in 1 Peter 1:3 and the psalmist's "living God" in Psalms 42:2?

• Based on the text of 1 Peter 1:3-5, how do I feel about the future dimensions of the living hope described in verses 4 and 5?

Conclusion

On the wall as one enters the college administration building of Palm Beach Atlantic College is a verse of Scripture from Isaiah 43:19, "Watch for the new thing I am going to do./It is happening already—you can see it now!" The rest of that verse, the part not quoted, says: "I will make a road through the wilderness/and give you streams of water there."

The living God is the One Who fills us with a living hope, one which no trials and tribulations can ever quench.

26

The Need for Truth

Truth or Consequences is actually the name of a small city in New Mexico. I don't know how the city got its name, but I have lived long enough to know that if humans don't do and tell the truth, they and their world will suffer the consequences.

Here is an example from my own experience. At the age of fourteen, I enlisted in the US Army. I lied about my age and told the recruiting sergeant I was seventeen. Way back then, a birth certificate was not required to enter the military. My mother very reluctantly signed for me, and thus added her lie to mine. The medical doctor who examined me said, "Are you sure you are seventeen; can you prove it?" This chain of lies continued for several years. Even though I stopped lying about my age many years ago, just this year—forty years later—I had to get a lawyer to help me clear up the mess.

I knew all along that it was wrong to lie. It bothered my conscience. The first week of basic training almost did me in. I was sorry I had lied, but I was too afraid of the possible consequences to tell the truth, until after I was discharged three-and-one-half years later. I not only told *a* lie and *many* lies about my age, I lived a lie, and I was in fact a liar. My lies and lying affected my character because truth is not merely something we tell; it is something we are and do. That's the reason we say persons have integrity who are truthful, do the truth, tell the truth, and in fact have the truth in them.

True, my lies did not have the same consequences as did those of the greedy Austrian wine dealers who in 1986 sweetened their products with diethylene glycol, an antifreeze component. Scores of vintners went bankrupt after the market for Austrian wine dried up. Some were convicted of fraud and drew prison sentences of up to ten years. Truth telling in this case might have been a matter of life and death.

German philosopher Rudolph Hofmann told the truth when he said, "Truth is the fundamental requirement of human life." Why place such a high premium on truth? Would not food be *the* fundamental requirement? Hofmann would agree that food is fundamental for the animal life that humans share. But this philosopher insists that distinctively human existence relies on "interhuman relationships and encounters," and these rely on truth.

John Bunyan's allegorical figure Mr. Valiant-for-truth might well have agreed with Hofmann's assessment of truth. Upon hearing that it was his time to die, Valiant-for-truth told his friends: "I do not repent me of all the trouble I have been at to arrive where I am . . . My marks and scars I carry with me, to be a witness for me, that I have fought His battles who now will be my rewarder."

Scripture Selection

Psalms 43:1-5

[1]O God, declare me innocent,/and defend my cause against the ungodly;/deliver me from lying and evil men!/[2]You are my protector;/why have you abandoned me?/Why must I go on suffering from the cruelty of my enemies?/

[3]Send your light and your truth;/may they lead me/and bring me back to Zion, your sacred hill,/and to your Temple, where you live./ [4]Then I will go to your altar, O God;/you are the source of my happiness./I will play my harp and sing praise to you,/O God, my God./

[5]Why am I so sad?/Why am I so troubled?/I will put my hope in God,/and once again I will praise him,/my savior and my God.

John 8:31-36

[31]So Jesus said to those who believed in him, "If you obey my teaching, you are really my disciples; [32]you will know the truth, and the truth will set you free."

[33]"We are the descendants of Abraham," they answered, "and we have never been anybody's slaves. What do you mean, then, by saying, 'You will be free'?"

[34]Jesus said to them, "I am telling you the truth: everyone who sins is a slave of sin. [35]A slave does not belong to a family permanently, but a son belongs there forever. [36]If the Son sets you free, then you will be really free."

Comments on Scripture Selection

Psalm 43 is a continuation of Psalm 42. Like Psalms 22, 51, and 109, it is a song of personal anguish. New Testament echoes of the psalm may be found in Mark 14:34 and John 12:27.

"Ungodly" in verse 1 literally reads: "unloved" or "people not compassionate." Possibly it meant those outside the divine covenant, and should be taken to mean that the enemies of the psalmist were the Assyrian or Babylonian invaders who had taken him into exile away from his homeland. Others, however, have suggested that it might have been a reference to Abasalom, David's son, who stirred up the rebellion that may have served as the context for the psalm. To whoever "ungodly" referred, it meant that the psalmist's enemies were pitiless; they expressed no deep affection and tender mercy.

Furthermore, these pitiless persons were "lying and evil men" (v. 1). The Revised Standard Version translates that part of verse 1 to read, "deceitful and unjust men." Therefore, in Psalm 43 the poet went beyond the depressing loneliness seen in Psalm 42 and reflected a sense of injustice. His enemies might well have been those who had borne false witness against him in some legal setting.

While this is a poem, and not a legal brief, in verse 1 the poet pleaded to God as though He were His judge, advocate, and bailiff all rolled up in one official: "Declare me innocent" (= judge), "defend my cause" (= advocate), "deliver me" (= bailiff). This kind of language would seem to fit the courtroom more than the altar (see v. 4).

Nevertheless, the psalmist did decisively turn his thoughts away from the courtroom to God's altar in verses 3-5. He seemed to realize that his thoughts would be solved ultimately in worship, rather than in court.

"Light" and "truth" in verse 3 were almost personified as God's twin messengers to guide the psalmist back to the house of God. Light in this context was equivalent to *favor* or *mercy*. "Truth" suggested God's faithfulness. "Lying and evil" (v. 1) are, of course, enemies of light and truth. But note that light and truth were not ends in themselves. They were prayed for in order to bring the pray-er back to Zion, that is, back to God.

John 8:31-36 tell even more about the truth which guides persons to God. "You will know the truth, and the truth will set you free" (v. 32), said Jesus to those Jews who believed in Him.

The Scripture selection from John may make better sense if you will go back at least to 8:21 and read straight through the end of chapter 8. Really 8:12-59 is probably a continuation of the dialogue begun in John 7:25.

Two groups of Jewish people might have been referred to in 8:31-36, those who heard Jesus and believed in Him (vv. 31-32), and those who heard Him and refused to believe He was the Son of God (vv. 33-36 *ff*.). Otherwise, the belief of those mentioned in verses 30-31 would have to be understood as very superficial indeed (see vv. 37 and 59). I take what is said about the Jews from verses 34-59 to refer to the hostile, openly scornful, unbelieving Jews who sought to kill Jesus (v. 37) and "picked up stones to throw at him" (v. 59).

Jesus' sayings in verses 32 and 36 should be set alongside each other. Truth here is the truth incarnated in Jesus Christ (see John 14:6; 1:14,17). Jesus claims to be God's agent for emancipation from the slavery of sin. Therefore, the freedom which Christ brings is primarily religious rather than political or social liberty.

Questions to Think About

• Do I agree with Rudolph Hofmann's conclusion that "Truth is the fundamental requirement of human life"?

• Can I think of a particular time when I did not tell the truth? If so, what were the consequences?

• Based on what has been said above about lying, and on what is said in Ephesians 4:15-16 about "speaking the truth in a spirit of love," why should anyone conclude that truth is something we are and do, as well as something we tell?

• Do I now have, or have I ever had, the kind of ungodly enemies described in Psalms 43, from whom I need(ed) to be declared innocent, defended, and/or delivered?

• What troubles (if any) do I have in the realm of truth or falsehood which I believe will ultimately be solved in worship rather than in some legal court?

• According to John 8:31-36, how does Jesus make persons "really free" (v. 36)?

• If I were summoned to die right now, could I say what John Bunyan's allegorical character Valiant-for-truth said to his friends (see the quotation)?

Conclusion

Judith Viorst in *Necessary Losses* told the story of a king who commissioned a great artist to paint the portrait of a famous holy man, renowned for his kindness and generosity. When the painting was unveiled with a flourish of trumpets, the face of the holy man in the painting was of someone brutish, cruel, and morally depraved. The king vowed he would have the artist's head. But the holy man intervened. "The portrait is true," he declared. "Before you stands the picture of the man I have struggled all my life not to become."

Is it possible that the truth we need most is the truth about ourselves?